AND I WILL BLESS THEM

By Roy Godwin

Release Date: August 1, 2023
ISBN: 978-0-8307-8546-9
Price: £14.99
Trim Size: 7 x 9
224 pages
Format: Paperback

Religion/Christian Living/Prayer

What people are saying about …

AND I WILL BLESS THEM

'Roy Godwin's story has impacted many thousands of lives, and in *And I Will Bless Them*, he invites us all to carry the blessing of God out into the world to transform communities.'

Pete Greig, author of *Red Moon Rising* and *God on Mute*

'This book will continually point you back to the Father, and rather than give you a list of things too, the writings are a deep dive to places in God that we all have access to. Prayer is a continual Invitation to a growing relationship with Jesus, and I pray as you read *And I Will Bless Them*, your hunger for the Word of God and His presence in and through your life will deepen and grow SO much that everyone in your world will be impacted.'

Darlene Zschech, pastor, worship leader, and composer

'I read Roy's first book, *The Grace Outpouring*, in 2011 and that book literally sparked a chain reaction of events that led to my church purchasing the iconic Bible College of Wales in Swansea and Pisgah Chapel in Loughor. So I am cautious about reading books by Roy because they will spark something prophetic in you and bring you down a path less trodden, but full of adventure. Roy's book *And I Will Bless Them* will surely encourage you to action. Be warned.'

Rev. Yang Tuck Yoong, senior pastor at Cornerstone Community Church, Singapore

'Roy is a storyteller; he loves to tell stories of how Jesus changed a life for eternity. Through his life and real encounters with people, Roy has taught me that God's desire is to bless me, my family and community. To recommend this book is to recommend a man who carries so much wisdom, insight and passion for seeing Jesus change our world through the practice of blessing.'

Jonathan Brown, president of Integrity Music

'As people who give leadership to international prayer initiatives, we have found the practice of blessing in Jesus' name, as presented by Roy in this book, significant from a missional perspective. Globally, teams of diverse nationalities have begun to minister through blessing, with the confidence it has an impact on the very places and spaces in which we live. It is a wonderful way to interact with families, friends and strangers in different settings, as most people regardless of background, are willing to receive words of blessing which opens the door for further ministry as God moves in their lives. We love to teach Roy's material to Operation Mobilisation teams as they walk out the practice of blessing in their locations around the world. The material is easy to follow and understand, and the discussion in our teams is rich as we learn how to speak blessings over people, communities, nations and the land on which we stand.'

Boyd and Ribka Williams, The Prayer Hub, OM International

'This book is filled up with sound and Spirit-filled theological insight which brings hope and new courage to minister the biblical secrets of blessing. Every part of the book has so many excellent examples of how people have had an encounter with the living God through the receiving of blessings from ordinary Christian people. There is a strong practical-theological insight found in this book that I think might change the lives of thousands of people around the world. I therefore recommend *And I Will Bless Them* to all Christians in different denominations and also to those who feel their ministry go out to people in the general society that long for a tangible touch from God. In the seven videos connected to the different passages of the book, Roy gives an excellent application to the written material and makes the reading of this book enriching and inspiring.'

Asbjørn Simonnes, PhD, professor at the University College of Theology and Governance, member of the steering committee of the national council of prayer in Norway and the theological advisory committee of Oase

'Reading this new book, *And I Will Bless Them*, was inspiring. This is a simple manuscript for the life of those learning to walk in the blessing of God. This book weaves the story and journey of blessing in a simple and practical pathway of learning that 'anyone can embrace in a walk of grace toward the way of truth revealing God's heart to bless and demonstrating the transformational impact of walking in the way of blessing. Bringing Course and the Story together in a book provides a way to multiply and expand blessing across nations.'

Mike Hey, international pioneer missionary and mentor, former director of OM Ships Ministry

'The Father's passionate desire to bless this world emanates from every page of this book. Roy communicates this ancient practice of the power of spoken blessing with love and authority, calling the sons and daughters of this generation to put into practice what we see our Father saying and doing. We have seen the fruit of blessing in our community and personal lives, heralding a transformative work of God that is undeniable. It's more than another model of prayer. It's about a sacred calling which applies to us all. I highly recommend this book to you. Don't just read it, but do it and see for yourself.'

Martin Dolan, director of Living Stones House of Prayer, Cyprus

ROY GODWIN

AUTHOR OF *THE GRACE OUTPOURING*

AN INTERACTIVE
GUIDE

Includes Seven-Session
Video Series

AND
I WILL
BLESS
THEM

RELEASING TRANSFORMATION THROUGH
THE SPOKEN BLESSING

DAVID C COOK®

transforming lives together

AND I WILL BLESS THEM
Published by David C Cook
4050 Lee Vance Drive
Colorado Springs, CO 80918 U.S.A.

Integrity Music Limited, a Division of David C Cook
Brighton, East Sussex BN1 2RE, England

The graphic circle C logo is a registered trademark of David C Cook.

ISBN 978-0-8307-8546-9
eISBN 978-0-8307-8552-0

© 2023 Roy Godwin
Portions of this book are from *The Way of Blessing*, published by David C Cook in 2016 © Roy Godwin, ISBN
978-0-78141442-5, and *The Blessings Course* by Roy Godwin and Dave Roberts © Roy Godwin Ministries.

The Team: Michael Covington, Jeff Gerke, James Hershberger, Jack Campbell, Susan Murdock
Cover Design: Micah Kandros
Cover Author Bio Photo: Kathryn Frost

Printed in the United States of America
First Edition 2023

1 2 3 4 5 6 7 8 9 10

041223

This book is dedicated to the memory and family of 'Uncle Charlie,' whose amazingly fruitful example of consistent blessing in China many years ago first inspired me to look afresh at the life-changing ministry of spoken blessing.

CONTENTS

ACKNOWLEDGEMENTS

I'd like to thank Michael Covington for first proposing this book, and Jeff Gerke and all the remarkable team at David C Cook who support me. Dave Roberts, for his skill and wisdom as he helps my writing; Christopher and Kathryn Frost, for their friendship and technical wizardry in design work and filming the videos; our many friends in Norway and Singapore; Mike and Ann Hey in Australia; Operation Mobilisation, and all those in many nations who are now walking in the Way of Blessing. Lastly, but always first in my heart, special thanks are reserved for Daphne, my wife, companion, fellow worker, and friend, who is indeed a gift from God, for showing great patience and mercy when I am in writing mode.

God is too great to need our exaggeration. This book contains numerous testimonies as spoken to us at various times. We want to be as accurate as possible. If the reader is aware of any error, please let us know, so that we may correct it in any future editions.

INTRODUCTION

In every generation, some truths are forgotten and others are remembered. In these days, God is calling His people to recover the age-old ministry of spoken blessing.

Jesus Christ came to save sinners. He also came to destroy the works of the evil one. The Gospels take time to show that Jesus not only declared the Father's words but also demonstrated the Father's work and authority in creation. We need to understand our calling, and the delegated authority we carry to proclaim the reality of God's kingdom, as our backdrop to the call to bless in Jesus' name.

In this interactive book, I present the ancient Christian practice of the spoken blessing. The ministry of spoken blessing introduces the present reality and power of the inbreaking kingdom of God to the moment. It conveys the power of God to shatter curses, for which it is the antidote, and releases captives.

The Bible teaches that we can bless people, communities, regions and nations, and even physical ground. Such blessings are *a ministry*. It's not simply about using nice words or creating liturgical forms. It's a transaction. Something happens when we speak blessing. It's undergirded by God's promise to come behind us when we bless … *and He will bless them.*

This book exists to help you explore and experience the ministry of blessing for yourself.

What really is a blessing as we're referring to it here? Is it something anyone can do, or is it reserved for a select few? Is there a magical formula to incant that releases the power of blessing?

Answers to those questions and many more will emerge as you journey through this book.

This book contains:

1. The Blessings Course video material—through the website link or QR code below, access a group leader's guide and seven video sessions with interactive questions that introduce the ministry of blessing. The video contents have been taught in many nations and have resulted in:

- Christians catching their purpose and seeing transformation take place around them.
- New small Christian communities coming into being.
- Churches, individual believers, and missional bodies building discipleship communities, with new people coming to faith as a result.

VIDEO SERIES ACCESS
Link: **DavidCCook.org/access**
Access code: **BlessThem**

**Scan this code with your mobile
device in camera mode.**

2. *Going Deeper* sections—these private readings enable you to explore more fully the theme of each session and what the Bible has to say. There is a useful template for each area of blessing to help you know how to shape a blessing and where to find scriptural pointers for the content.

Note: *And I Will Bless Them* is designed to be used ideally in a small group of two to twelve people. Individuals are encouraged to find someone else to do it with, if possible. The Going Deeper sections are for individual reading.

For pastors and leaders: please use this book with small groups. Do not use it congregationally, because the interaction would be lost.

When you have been through the contents of the book, you will be confident:

- That God's deep desire is to bless you.
- That He is calling you to become effective with the ministry of blessing.
- What God's will is for your community.
- Who and what to bless.

- Who and what you must never bless.
- How to bless people, communities, regions and nations, and physical ground.
- How to walk in the way of blessing.

Apart from this book, you will need two items for the journey: a Bible and a pen to make notes as you go.

The recommended sequence for you to enjoy *And I Will Bless Them* is this:

- Gather as a group and watch the video session.
- One person should act as group leader or facilitator. (Download the Leader's Guide provided at the QR code above.)
- As a group, discuss the questions that go with the video.
- Later, individually, read the subsequent pages in personal private time to go even deeper into the theme of each session.

The material is designed for group use, but you can do all of it, including the videos, on your own as well.

The ministry of blessing is part of every believer's role. You may be male or female, young or old, rich or poor, from any background, educated or not, of any colour and any political persuasion. It doesn't matter—if you have placed your faith and trust in the Lord Jesus, you are equally invited. There is life and purpose for you within the kingdom of God, which is breaking in now and will be seen in its fullness in the future.

Individual Christians of any age, church leaders, small group leaders, youth leaders, pastors and leaders of outreach and mission should find *And I Will Bless Them* challenging, exciting and eminently practical.

Prelude

GOD'S BLESSINGS RELEASED

On our way home after I had spoken at a conference on the southern English coast, my phone screen lit up with a message from the hosting church. I had encouraged the attendees to intercede for the three towns that form their conurbation, that God would display Himself to the people and draw them to Jesus. We'd stood together, and I'd led them in a simple prayer. We had then spoken blessings over the inhabitants and blessed their ability to hear and recognise the voice of God.

The message explained that on Sunday afternoon, the youth leader had been in the church building preparing for the youth service to be held later, when a couple of youngsters had wandered in. She chatted with them and explained that they could come to events but that their mum would have to meet with her first and book them in.

To her surprise, they returned very quickly—together with their mum, who wanted to know what this big industrial building on an industrial estate was. When the youth leader explained that it was a church, she was amazed and asked what type of church it was. Was it lively?

Then it was the youth leader's turn to be amazed, when the woman explained that she had just told her best friend that she had heard God speak to her about going to church. 'And here I am, in a church, just down the street from me, and I didn't even know that it was a church. Can I come to services?'

When we walk in the way of blessing, this sort of story becomes quite common.

Everything in this book is written for *you*. Life, joy, peace, belonging, purpose, power, healing and restoration—all are available to you. God invites you to step in and taste and see for yourself that the Lord is good. He will then lead you on a journey of releasing His blessing to others. The purpose of this book is to help you make a good start.

The following stories illustrate what God does through spoken blessing. I hope they encourage you as you begin your own journey in the way of blessing.

Stories of Blessing

We were at a harvest festival meal in a local church when a man suddenly walked over from one of the other tables, looking very excited. He told us that the BBC Welsh language radio and television programmes had, in an interview, just referred to the retreat centre which we led at the time. This was news to us. We were not aware of any current reason that might cause such a mention.

We discovered that the interview was with a certain salesman who had come to the centre hoping to sell us a commercial photocopier. After a coffee, he had discussed our printing needs with my secretary. Once he finished his sales pitch, he was surprised to be offered a tour of the centre. He really didn't want to do the tour, but if that's what it took to sell the photocopier, he thought, he was happy to go along with it.

As usual, the tour concluded in the chapel. There, my secretary explained that it was our normal practice to offer to bless people before they left. The salesman again reluctantly decided that a blessing would be an acceptable price to pay if it led to a sale.

We had trained our staff, when with somebody who was not yet a Christian, to say something like, 'I bless you in Jesus' name that you might come to know everything you need to know in order to live the fullest life possible as the person you were created to be.'

My secretary, as yet unaware of what had happened, left him in the chapel so God could do whatever He wanted to do. The man later testified that the moment he was blessed he felt as though he had been struck by lightning. His life was ripped open and exposed.

After some time had passed, he set out for home and drove down into the valley, where he stopped to look up at the hillside. It was a very gloomy day with black clouds and low fog. Just at that moment, a single sunbeam broke through and focussed directly on the high cross on the hill. He sat there in his car, transfixed by it. Somehow, he said, he suddenly understood what Jesus had done for him.

Once home, he announced to his wife that he was going to church. His wife, quite surprised by this turn of events, said she would go with him. There, he made a life-changing commitment to the Lord Jesus, closely followed by a similar commitment from his wife.

The reason the story so fascinated the media was that the salesman turned out to be a national hero. He had captained the Welsh International Rugby Squad (the national sport) when a younger man and had led them through two World Cups. In the radio and TV interviews, he described how the Lord had brought about a life that was thoroughly changed, how his relationships had changed and how his business practices and attitudes towards people had been transformed. This is the fruit of a changed life—a changed person with a new heart and a new spirit.

His testimony is making an impact on many people because of his background, his name and his fame. Several years on, he is still repeating this story of a truly life-changing blessing.

One of my favourite emails arrived from a Central African nation where I had been teaching missional prayer and blessing, together with acts of mercy. The message was from a significant leader, who wrote, 'Thank you for bringing this teaching to us. We pray that it will multiply across the whole of Africa because *wherever our people have started doing it, the kingdom of God has rushed in with power.'*

Coffee time was over, and I was hurrying back into the hall where I had been teaching on blessing in the snowy north of Norway. Timing was important because the talks were being filmed, and I was in a rush.

Suddenly, a woman stepped into my path and asked if she could speak with me. I think I looked at her with some surprise as I explained that we needed to keep to the timetable. Could she speak with me at lunchtime, I asked? 'No,' she said, 'it's important that I tell you something now.' Slightly irritated, I asked her what was so urgent. She seemed to almost stand on tiptoe with excitement as she yelled, 'Tell them it works here! Tell them it's all true and it works!'

Now rather bemused, I asked her what she was referring to. 'Everything,' she said. 'It all works here!' Out of the corner of my eye, I could see a man hurrying my way to urge me to come in, so again I asked her what it was that worked.

She excitedly explained that she and her husband had started to pray and bless her city in the manner as described in this book. She had my full attention then. I asked what had happened that had caused her to say that it worked here. She answered that she couldn't tell me because I wouldn't believe it. She said that even she and her husband couldn't believe what was happening, because such amazing change was taking place before their eyes in the city and in people's lives.

'Tell them it works anywhere,' she said. And she was right ...

After a church leader in Australia had spoken with me, he gathered his people on a Saturday to purposely bless the building and the grounds. The next day, they were surprised by the number of first-time visitors who attended their service. Several days later, they held their weekly children's gathering and were amazed when twice the previous number showed up.

I was speaking in a one-day conference and introduced the audience to the ministry of blessing. Having taught from the Scriptures, I said that there was a very big difference between speaking blessing and ministering blessings. I described the difference between interceding for God to bless and *speaking* blessings.

While speaking to a group, I invited a woman to come forward to act as a blessing-receiving example. I said to everyone, 'My desire is that this lady should be blessed.' I wasn't aware at that point that she was a pastor's wife. I then turned away and started to pray. I said, 'Father, You're the God of blessings. I ask You to come because of Jesus and release mighty blessings on the lady standing behind me. Amen.'

I asked the congregation what I had done. 'You've blessed her,' was their response. I said, 'Well, actually, no, I haven't. I've petitioned the Father. I've asked *Him* to bless her. When we bless somebody directly, it's quite different.'

I turned around, faced the woman, and said, 'I bless you in the name of Jesus, that the Father may bless you. I bless you that the peace and the joy of God may come upon you and wash through every part of your being, physically, mentally, socially and spiritually.'

Her eyes filled up a little, and she thanked me, then sat down. It was only at the end of the day that she came up to me and said, 'Do you know, it's quite amazing; I have suffered from chronic, constant back pain for twenty years, and it disappeared the moment you spoke that blessing.'

Six hundred people from churches across a large English town gathered for a day's training on the ministry of blessing. We connected it with focussed intercession for the town, specifically crying out for the kingdom of God to be released.

Around a year later, the organising pastor contacted us to say that a well-known newspaper had published a story concerning the rapid improvement in the status of that town. People were happier and crime had decreased. The local economy had prospered so much that if you wanted to start a business, this was the place to do it. A greater proportion of start-ups succeeded there than anywhere else in England. There were also fewer bankruptcies.

Day by day we are blessed as we receive such stories of people in many nations powerfully speaking the blessing of God, impacting people, communities, regions and nations and even physical ground.

Who are these world changers? Just ordinary people who are learning to walk with an extraordinary Father in the power of the Holy Spirit.

Whoever you are and wherever you are, God loves you and longs to reveal more of Himself to you. He longs to transform your life and release spoken blessing into you and also through you, impacting others and changing the world, one step at a time.

The rest of this book is designed to help you through your journey of discovery.

PART I

PERSONAL FOUNDATIONS FOR THE WAY OF BLESSING

Session 1

THE GOD WHO BLESSES

Gather with your group for your first session. When everyone is introduced and comfortable, work through the material below. Go slowly and reflectively. Honour each other's comments. Watch the video at the recommended point, then continue working through the questions together.

Scripture

> The LORD said to Moses, 'Tell Aaron and his sons, "This is how you are to bless the Israelites. Say to them:
>
> ""The LORD bless you
>   and keep you;

the LORD make his face shine on you
   and be gracious to you;
the LORD turn his face towards you and give you peace.'"

   'So they will put my name on the Israelites, and I will bless them.' (Num. 6:22–27)

Prayer

- **Individual:** If you're reading this alone, sing or reflect on the well-known hymn below. As you hear these perhaps familiar words, you could close your eyes and savour what they tell us about the work of God amongst us.
- **Group:** If you're reading this as part of a group, the words below could be read slowly by one person or they could be sung together if the group knows the hymn well. The best way is for four people to be given a verse each—this will bring variety in delivery. As you hear these perhaps familiar words, you could close your eyes and savour what they tell us about the work of God amongst us.

Love divine, all loves excelling,
joy of heaven, to earth come down,
fix in us thy humble dwelling,
all thy faithful mercies crown.
Jesus, thou art all compassion,
pure, unbounded love thou art.
Visit us with thy salvation;
enter every trembling heart.

Breathe, oh, breathe thy loving Spirit
into every troubled breast.
Let us all in thee inherit;
let us find the promised rest.
Take away the love of sinning;
Alpha and Omega be.
End of faith, as its beginning,
set our hearts at liberty.

Come, Almighty, to deliver,
let us all thy life receive.
Suddenly return, and never,
nevermore thy temples leave.
Thee we would be always blessing,
serve thee as thy hosts above,
pray and praise thee without ceasing,
glory in thy perfect love.

Finish, then, thy new creation;
pure and spotless let us be.
Let us see thy great salvation
perfectly restored in thee.
Changed from glory into glory,
till in heaven we take our place,
till we cast our crowns before thee,
lost in wonder, love and praise.

Suggested statement from the group leader: 'Today, we will examine the foundations of why we are called to be a people of blessing and how this is rooted in the character and the will of God. Roy Godwin has some teaching that will help us reflect on this.'

Play Video: SESSION ONE

We encourage you to take notes as you watch the video. Feel free to use the space under the Your Notes header following this paragraph. Note anything that you find especially helpful or that provokes you to examine the way you view what it means to love God and to follow Jesus in the world today.

Your Notes

Review

What helped or provoked you in what Roy shared in the video? Underline the key points in the notes you made. If you are part of a group, share together, if that would be helpful.

Reflect

Do you have any additional insights about the character of God and why He would desire to bless us? What Scripture stories, verses or principles spring to your mind as you reflect on these topics? Write them in your notes. If you are part of a group, share together, if that would be helpful.

Focus

- **Individual:** The following Key Insights section provides supporting scriptures and a deeper look into the content of this session to supplement what you have already noted.

- **Group:** If you're studying as a group, your group leader will now summarise some of the things you have shared together. Be ready to note any additional points he or she may make that could be helpful to you. The following Key Insights section provides supporting scriptures and a deeper look into the content of this session. Use this material to supplement what you have already noted and to aid further discussion. You may find it useful for personal reflection at a later date as well.

Key Insights

Psalm 136—Roy referred to the idea of the Hebrew word *chesed*, the steadfast love of God. Psalm 136 is a poetic, historic and majestic expression of *chesed*. You may want to read some verses from this psalm.

Mark 1:11—God publicly affirmed that Jesus is His Son, who brings Him much joy. Note that this was *before* Jesus had commenced His ministry. It had nothing to do with performance. In the same way, God wants to bless you just because His desire is to bless His children.

John 5:19—To understand God and His love for us, we must look to Jesus. In this key verse, Jesus tells us that He does only what He sees the Father doing. Roy reflected on this in the video.

Luke 15:11–32—Jesus also tells the story of a gracious father in the story we know as the parable of the prodigal son. This father sets aside his dignity to run to the returning son, welcomes him home, and protects him. The ministry of Jesus and His teaching is the cornerstone and the key foundation of how we can start to fully understand God.

1 John 3:16—'This is how we know what love is: Jesus Christ laid down his life for us. And we ought to lay down our lives for our brothers and sisters.' God wants to bless us because love is the essence of His character.

Love Is Active

Love seeks a transformation of life's circumstances and a return to the intent that God has for us. When Jesus blesses people:

- The blind see.
- The paralysed walk.
- The deaf hear.
- The feverish are healed.
- The unclean are accepted.
- The dead come to life.
- The demonised are set free.
- The guilty are forgiven.
- The outsider is welcomed.
- The hungry and naked are clothed, fed and watered.
- Prisoners are visited.
- The poor have good news preached to them.
- And so much more …

Blessing Is Central to the Lord's Prayer

'Thy will be done in earth, as it is in heaven' (Matt. 6:10 KJV) affirms that God desires to bring heaven to earth. The blessing of God will flow into our lives as God's will for our wholeness comes to pass.

Blessing Is at the Centre of the Mission Mandate

When Jesus sent out His disciples in bands of two, He told them that as they entered a house, they should declare, 'Peace to this house.' The word *shalom* used by Jesus here speaks of wholeness, peace and restoration. Jesus made the blessing of God a forerunner of the declaration of the kingdom of God.

Your Notes

Jesus made the blessing of God
a forerunner of the declaration
of the kingdom of God.

Prayer

As we conclude our session, we turn to prayer, talking to the God who blesses and declaring our own blessing and thankfulness towards Him. You can use the following prayer and/or the prayer idea below it.

Lord, open our lips to bless You

And our mouths shall declare Your praise.

Blessed are You, gracious God;

We will give You glory and praise forever!

The LORD is my portion, says my soul,

Therefore, I will put my hope in Him.

Prayer Idea

In a moment of silence, think of an aspect of God that has been a comfort, encouragement or inspiration to you. Or you might want to think of the biblical names of the Father, Jesus and the Holy Spirit and what they say of the character of God.

- **Individual:** Speak aloud your prayers towards God, expressing your thankfulness for the life, beauty, creativity and generosity that we have just reminded ourselves are found in Him.
- **Group:** Speak aloud your prayers towards God, expressing your thankfulness for the life, beauty, creativity and generosity that we have just reminded ourselves are found in Him.

Life Activity

When you get up from this study and before the next session, take this verse as your watchword:

> Bless the LORD, O my soul;
> And all that is within me, bless His holy name!
> Bless the LORD, O my soul,
> And forget not all His benefits. (Ps. 103:1–2 NKJV)
> [benefits = all the good things He does for me]

As your group dismisses and you all go back to your lives, remember to look for the life, beauty, creativity and generosity of God in all the situations, places and people that you encounter this week. Send up a prayer to God, thanking Him for His blessing.

Session 1:
Going
Deeper

THE GOD WHO BLESSES

Further Material for Personal Reading

He glanced nervously in his mirror, worried that his friend might die at any moment. He had agreed to take her to a prayer meeting, something he was not familiar with at all. He was concerned, having been told by her doctors that she might die on the way. But his quick glances in the strategically angled mirror suggested that she was coping well with the journey.

In fact, she was coping much better than anybody could have imagined.

After a long drive, he found the car park beside the church in the remote valley near the retreat centre where we lived and worked. Having parked the car, he went round to lift her out. But she informed him that she was going to walk in. He was taken aback, but she instructed him to let her hold on to him. She said to herself, *I got here, and God is going to meet me.*

I knew nothing of this. A few moments later, though, I sensed the breath of God as we were singing the first song of our worship time at the monthly Prayer Day. We paused, and I shared with the group what I believed God was putting on my heart: 'You've come here today with desperation, and it's your very last hope. There will be nowhere else to turn—there is no hope anywhere else. You believe that during Prayer Day you will have an encounter with God which is going to fundamentally change your life.'

I looked out over those gathered. 'This is what God says: "It's not going to happen." Why? Because He's already met with you on the way here. And if you will just stop now and say, "Thank You," you will receive the fullness of what God is giving you. If that's you, I suggest that you say, "Thank You, Lord," and by faith receive what He has given. As for the rest of us, we'll carry on with our worship.'

When we broke for lunch, a woman came almost running down the central aisle to the front. 'I want you to know that I'm sure I'm the person that you had that word for,' she said.

'Well, that's wonderful,' I responded. 'Did you say, "Thank You"?'

'Yes, I did.'

I asked if she had received by faith what God wanted to give her. She said she believed she had. I blessed her in Jesus' name to walk in the fullness of it, then asked to be excused and went off to get my lunch.

A few days later, the phone started ringing. Church leaders and pastors from Cardiff, our capital city, wanted to know about the amazing miracle that had happened one hundred miles away at our Prayer Day. Well, we had prayed for many people on Prayer Day, and I wasn't aware that anything particularly outstanding had occurred on that day. I asked them to tell me what they had been hearing, and I was put in touch with one of our friends who also knew the woman at the heart of this miracle story. I called, and an astonishing story emerged.

Chrissie had been ill with myalgic encephalomyelitis (ME, also called chronic fatigue syndrome) for many years. She had multiple health challenges and was being rushed to a high-dependency unit at her local hospital several times a year to help keep her going and deal with urgent health issues.

She had a friend, Ken, who throughout her illness had been supportive and practical. Occasionally, she would want to venture out to see the countryside, but the last of those car trips had ended abruptly when she collapsed on the way. The paramedics had to resuscitate her at the side of the road.

Sometime later, when she asked Ken to take her to a retreat centre, she was nearing the end of her life—her body had moved into organ failure. It was a serious situation.

Someone had given her a copy of *The Grace Outpouring*—the story of how the presence of God was touching many lives at an isolated retreat centre in Pembrokeshire, Wales. She read it, and as she did so, her faith was stirred. She began to believe that if she could visit, God would meet her there and would heal her.

She was very clear in her own mind. It was not about the team at the centre and how effective their prayer might be. She believed that God Himself would meet her there. She asked Ken to take time off work and help her get to our remote valley. He remonstrated with her, 'You know you can't even get out of the bed to go to the bathroom—you can't go anywhere. You're near the end.'

She did not actually know where exactly the centre was, but she implored him to grant her this one last wish. He looked us up on the internet and was horrified to discover we were one hundred miles away, much of which was cross-country on single-track lanes. He told her this, but she insisted that she wanted to go.

Ken remained deeply wary. He called her doctors and shared with them what she was proposing. They believed she would die during the journey. They were also of the opinion she would die very soon anyway. They hinted that granting her this final wish might be a good thing to do for a friend and wished him good luck with his choice. He checked our website and agreed to take her to our next Prayer Day, as long as she slept the night before.

When he arrived in the morning, he asked whether she'd slept. She said no, so he said he wouldn't take her. She insisted, and he then decided to take her anyway. He carried her out and settled her in the car. He began to weep. He felt sure that this would be the last time that he would see her alive—she was going to die in his car.

He got into the car and adjusted the mirror so he could see when she passed away. When that happened, he would turn round and go to the hospital. He set off on the two-and-a-half-hour journey. What he couldn't understand when he looked in the mirror was that the farther he went and the closer he got to the Prayer Day venue, the healthier she looked.

Once they arrived, to his complete shock she said she would walk in if he would hold her up. Just as she came through the door, she heard the words God prompted me to share. Her heartfelt response was 'Yes' and she felt immediately strengthened. So much so that she almost ran the length of the hall to me right then to say it was she to whom God had spoken. I didn't know her at all, and there were no clues that a physical miracle was underway, unless you knew how very ill she had been. They drove back to Cardiff that night.

The next morning, Ken went to her home to see her. He rang the bell, then used his key to go inside. He called her name, but there was no reply. He looked in the kitchen, but there was no sign of anything or anybody. He knocked on her bedroom door and called her name. There was no reply. He knocked three times and said, 'Unless you call out, I'm going to open the door.' There was no answer, so he opened the door, nervous about what he might find. There was no one there.

He was really worried now, because he thought she had died in the night and the body had been removed. He was quite upset. Suddenly the front door opened and in walked Chrissie. He felt a mixture of relief and anger. 'What are you doing and where have you been?' he demanded to know. She told him she'd been for a walk by the river. He was incredulous. 'You can't walk—you're not *able* to walk!'

'Ken,' she gently replied, 'God met me yesterday and He healed me. Do you remember?'

In the coming weeks, the day-to-day reality of what had happened to his friend began to really dawn for Ken. He went to a local Alpha course, an introduction to Christianity. His life changed. Ken and Chrissie eventually married, and now they're actively involved in ministry themselves.

Pause for a moment. Chrissie's story is not an isolated one. God still acts today in the way that He did in the life of Jesus, who heralded the good news that people could discover life, peace, healing and joy as a gift from God. But even as you reflect on what you just read, other details from the story may be speaking to you.

Did you notice that I blessed Chrissie after our short discussion? Can anyone bless someone in the name of Jesus?

Before we can get into that, we need to understand something of the character of God and how He desires to deepen our understanding of Him as a bedrock foundation for the things we might do and say in His name. For some, their initial steps on this journey start in doubt, not resolute faith.

In Chrissie's case, when God brought heaven to earth to heal her, there was a ripple effect which expanded until it touched the life of a sceptical minister. Months later, I shared Chrissie's story at an event. A vicar in the congregation burst into tears and couldn't stop. The story awoke an interest in him about the present-day presence of God and the work of the Holy Spirit. He found it very difficult to accept the story as being true. So he decided to attend one of our Prayer Days for himself.

Months later, he eventually came. He had never driven on the sort of narrow lanes that we have in rural Pembrokeshire. He was late and a bit lost. He ultimately parked his car near another person's that had arrived just before him.

As he got out, a young woman greeted him and asked, 'Do you come here every month?' She discovered it was his first time ever. She then asked what had brought him here, and he explained that he'd heard the story of a woman who had been healed on the way to a monthly Prayer Day. He was honest and said he couldn't understand it, but he knew that he had to come and see for himself. She said, 'My name is Chrissie, and I'm that person.'

He had a great encounter with God that day. God opened his eyes to see His compassion.

When it comes to blessings, we embrace the Father's love and compassion as our foundation. We view the world through His eyes because of His promise: 'The LORD is compassionate and gracious, slow to anger, abounding in love.… As a father has compassion on his children, so the LORD has compassion on those who fear him' (Ps. 103:8, 13).

Psalm 103 also tells us that He has crowned us with love and compassion. A crown is a symbol of authority. God will use those speaking from a position of love and compassion to bring blessing to the lives of many. Sometimes, however, we all need to have our eyes opened and our vision enlarged.

Is Our Gospel Too Small?

We are all prone to reducing life to short sayings. In our mainstream culture, people may say some of the following: 'Get what you can while you can.' 'Every man for himself.' 'Science offers the hope of a new and peaceful future.' 'New hope for a transformed world.' 'Equal society through our creed.' These ideas come and go, flourishing for a while and then being undone by genocide, nuclear bombs and a horror at a society that cares little for others.

Over the years, I have been challenged by the title of a book by J. B. Phillips: *Your God Is Too Small.* That little phrase stays with you. In my own life, I began to realise that the good news about Jesus I was preaching had become too small.

Perhaps we as Christians are also prone to one-sentence gospel summaries. We explain that Jesus came to pay the price of sin so we might all go to heaven. We might even have created an expanded outline like this:

- God created the earth.
- God fellowshipped with humanity.
- We fell through sin.
- Separation, spoiling and disjointedness were the results.
- Jesus came as the Saviour.
- At the cross, He paid the price for our rebellion, bearing our sins for us.
- We are now forgiven.
- One day, we will be with Him.

Everything in that outline above is gloriously true. And yet … it falls short of the breadth of the gospel proclaimed by the prophets, the poets, Jesus Himself and the apostles. It is purely transactional and ignores the life and teaching of Jesus about other matters.

Jesus died in our place, we say. Wonderfully true! But limiting the good news to this is to ignore the teaching of Jesus concerning the kingdom of God. It says nothing of the overwhelming love of the Father which moves God in self-giving steadfast love and compassion towards you and me in a never-ending torrent.

'"My steadfast love shall not depart from you, and my covenant of peace shall not be removed," says the LORD, who has compassion on you' (Isa. 54:10 ESV).

The astonishing, world-changing fact is that God loves you and me. He woos us into a relationship founded on love and compassion. We can believe with all our heart in the 'gospel outline' listed above. But it becomes alive only when we step into the personal relationship of love and compassion that the Father has committed Himself to. He is crazy about you! He wants to do you good!

Perhaps the most famous story ever told is known to us as the story of the prodigal son. Two thousand years after the telling, there are numerous famous paintings and books about it, and biblical commentators and scholars still get their teeth into it. Socially and culturally speaking, this story (with its many strands) was an utter offence to those who first heard it. The legal parameters of the story were clear: the son was a disgrace to himself, his family and to the community. But Jesus told of grace.

Here is one way of summarising the father in this story: He wasn't anything like your expectations. This was not a father who was brooding with anger over his rebellious child. He was not vengeful, biding his time for judgement to come.

This was a father who was aching with love for his lost child. He was a grieving father who:

- Was longing and looking for his son.
- Threw propriety to the wind and disgracefully ran to meet him when he returned.
- Shockingly embraced him, although he was unclean.
- Swept away the son's words—because he knew the son's heart.
- Rejoiced, because his son who had been lost was now found.

- Forgave the past and restored his son's status, even though he had squandered everything he had received.
- Publicly challenged expectations of social behaviour in order to protect his son.

What kind of father is this? He is an illustration of the God and Father of our Lord Jesus Christ. The One who has welcomed you and me. The One who has always loved you and longed for you, dreaming of putting forgiveness to work in your life and mine, of redemption and of an eternity of unstoppable love.

This father looks exactly like Jesus, who is the radiance of the glory of God and the exact imprint of His nature. 'When God raised up his servant, he sent him first to you to bless you' (Acts 3:26).

Jesus utterly confounded the religious expectations of what the Messiah would be like. He challenged orthodoxy and hypocrisy. He also challenged the cultural framework where religion had shaped it. He sat and spoke with the Samaritan woman at the well; He physically touched lepers and welcomed outcasts; He forgave sinners; He ate and relaxed with traitorous tax collectors and sinners; and He was bold to embrace the ceremonially unclean. When we see the Son, we do indeed see the Father.

I cannot begin to adequately describe what all this means to me personally. By His choice, His saving work and my assent, I am a sinner saved by grace. He has given me the power to become a child of God. I am free of condemnation. I have a future hope that stands rock solid on a solid Rock. I am called into a relationship with the Creator Redeemer King. I am known and made acceptable to Him, by Him. How crazy is that? He longs for and loves to enjoy my attention and company. He takes delight in me. Even when I stink with sin and shame, He embraces me in His Father's hug.

And how do I know this is true? I look at the cross and see the nails, the sword-inflicted wound, the crown and the blood, and I see my Father's love for me openly displayed. The spirit of adoption within me bears witness, crying out, 'Abba! Father!' The Word of God is alive, and the promises are assured, finding their 'Yes' in Him.

As I walk on through life, I know that should the earth shake or should disaster overwhelm the world, God's two gifts will still forever be tied to my ankles: His goodness and mercy, which will follow me for endless days (see Ps. 23:6).

This, of course, is the invitation to each one of us. The prodigal's father is even now looking, grieving with love, waiting for the opportunity to run and welcome you. Surely this is the Father we have always longed for. A Father who loves and gives, who loves and gives again and again. Who, having given His Son for us, will continue to freely give us all things. Who calls us and resources us, choosing to display His love and glory through our lives. Yes, ours!

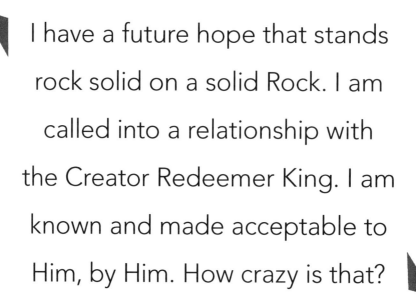

I have a future hope that stands rock solid on a solid Rock. I am called into a relationship with the Creator Redeemer King. I am known and made acceptable to Him, by Him. How crazy is that?

God has passionately committed Himself to have mercy on us and heal us, to restore us and make us whole. But we don't always grasp this, despite the clear and consistent witness of Scripture. If we're honest, many of us wrestle with it. We're hoping He heals, but we're not sure. I just love the way God moves and makes it very clear that the story is about Him and not us.

So if the story, including the story of blessing, is about God and not us, does that mean the deaf can still come to hear, and the blind begin to see, and the lame learn to walk even today?

The Deaf Hear

Two guests who were friends of my wife, Daphne, were staying at the centre. On their final day, we invited them to come and have a coffee and a few minutes' fellowship with us before they left. One of them was distressed, breaking the news that he had lost his hearing aids.

Daphne sent the housekeepers over to search their room, but the hearing aids couldn't be found. They thought about their activity that morning, but it was really limited to their room. Common areas were searched exhaustively just in case. It was as if his hearing aids had physically disappeared.

I asked him what the extent of the difficulty would be that this loss would cause. He told me he couldn't hear a thing without them. I immediately registered that he was hearing something! He was distressed, however—he explained that he couldn't hear the television news without it being on full volume, even when had his hearing aids in. He was concerned that life would become very quiet until he got replacements.

'How long have you had this condition?' was my next enquiry. He had been very hard of hearing for seven years. I lowered my voice a little more and noted that Daphne understood what was happening; she was grinning. I asked him something else very quietly, which he responded to, and then I whispered to him, and he looked at me as if to say, what on earth are you doing whispering? He answered me. We allowed this to go on for a little while before he suddenly realised that he was hearing absolutely perfectly. And he still does to this very day.

The presence of God had touched him with healing.

The Blind See

One night in the meeting room during evening prayers, the Holy Spirit came in power. Mary, one of our visitors, fell to her face onto the floor asking why her eyes hurt so much. Sylvia, the wife of the volunteer leading the meeting, reached down and raised Mary up by the elbow and said, 'Come and stand with me.' She then gently prompted her: 'Mary, open your eyes.'

Mary looked and turned and whispered into Sylvia's ear, 'You see that man over there? I love his shirt!' Everybody heard the whisper, and the whole room erupted in praise.

Why? Because Mary was blind. Earlier in life, she had had only partial sight in one eye. But now as she turned and surveyed the room, she was able to recognise her husband. 'Look at the size of the grin on my husband's face!' she joyfully informed the room.

This story is powerful in and of itself, but it becomes more poignant as the story behind the story unfolds. Mary and her husband, Peter, had not been Christians for very long—two or three years at the most. She was blind in both eyes. They had a strong desire to mark their forthcoming wedding anniversary with a special short holiday.

They spoke to their pastor, who suggested (a bit tongue in cheek) that if they wanted to go somewhere quiet and isolated with beautiful surroundings and where nothing ever happened, perhaps they should try a certain retreat centre in Wales!

The lodging rooms at our retreat centre were fully booked, so they decided to camp locally. When they arrived after a long journey, they visited the centre briefly and met a few guests, who welcomed them and spoke excitedly of the things that God was doing there.

That quite astonished them. They knew nothing about this aspect of the place that they had been directed to. One of the guests suggested that they read *The Grace Outpouring*, which described some of the background to what God was doing. Back at the campsite, they downloaded the book onto Mary's phone. Peter topped up his worship-song collection on his phone.

The next day was their wedding anniversary, and they travelled to the centre for Morning Prayers. Having misunderstood the time, they arrived exactly as it ended. To their amazement, instead of being mildly disappointed, they were emotionally churned about it but couldn't understand why.

It was a lovely sunny day, so they wandered down to the high cross and lay on the grass nearby. He listened to worship and she listened to *The Grace Outpouring* audiobook. She was simply amazed. Miracle stories in this day and age were new to her.

They went off for Midday Prayers, had lunch, and then went back and lay on the grass. Peter listened to more worship and she listened to the second part of *The Grace Outpouring*. It had been a mundane but peaceful day. Then they went in for Evening Prayers.

Daphne and I were away that day. Normally, a team member would take prayers in that situation, but Bryn and Sylvia, a couple of volunteers who'd been with us for three months, were setting off back to Canada the next day and this was their last evening. So I'd asked them if they would like to take the Evening Prayers; they were thrilled.

An awful lot of people were packed into the meeting room—the chapel we often use would not have held them all. There was a moment in our Evening

Prayers when we would say together: 'Lord, wherever spiritual, physical or emotional darkness touches me, I trust You to lighten it.'

As the people prayed those words, the Holy Spirit fell on the room in power. People were calling out and weeping and bowing down, but Mary grabbed her eyes, saying, 'My eyes hurt, my eyes hurt! What's going on with my eyes?' She fell on her knees, crying out that her eyes really hurt. Bryn, who was leading, wondered what he'd done wrong. He was quite upset, but his wife, Sylvia, was saying, 'Lord, this is fantastic! What a wonderful way to have our last evening here.'

Mary received her sight during that outpouring of the Holy Spirit. When Daphne and I got back, around ten in the evening, we listened to a message on the answering machine that sounded a little hysterical: 'I've seen it, I've seen it, I've seen it!' I couldn't understand what on earth it was about, but after playing it a number of times, I recognised a Canadian accent, and I wondered if it was Sylvia. I rang Sylvia and Bryn.

'Thank goodness you've rung,' was their immediate response.

I asked if all was well. It became clear that they were shaken by something that had happened, so I told them I was coming straightaway. I charged off, really concerned, and found them unable to sit down, pacing up and down and unsure what to do with themselves.

They were in a state of wonder. 'We saw it; we saw it. We have seen somebody who was blind receive their sight!' Bryn and Sylvia had asked Mary whether she and Peter would stay on until the next day so that I could meet them, and I was so grateful for that.

First thing the next morning, I was able to talk to Mary and Peter. I learned that as a little child she had lost her sight in one eye and then had fading eyesight in the other. Eight or nine years previously, her sight had gone completely. She had been totally blind.

As I looked at her now, her eyes were never still. They were looking everywhere, which slightly concerned me. I mentioned this and she explained what was happening. 'I'm going to have to learn how to control that and focus, but I can't stop looking at everything. There's colour, light and shape everywhere.' She was drinking in the beauty outside, the colour of the carpet, the sun shining on the table and highlighting the different grain. She couldn't stop for a moment.

Mary and Peter explained that back at home they had several young children. Obviously, they wanted to return home to their children, but they didn't seem to be in a hurry, and that confused me. So I asked why they were not in a hurry to get home.

They said they would go and see their pastor first and talk to him. That didn't make sense to me, so again I asked why. They explained that they were actually frightened of seeing the children, because everything would be so different. Mary would be seeing her younger children for the first time ever. She'd seen the older children as infants eight years previously, but with limited vision.

But what if she didn't like how they looked? How they dressed? How they ate their food? Their mannerisms and habits? All the things that she had never seen—how would she cope? Would her sense of loving them change when she saw them?

I felt that was a really helpful reality check and it put a new spotlight on the stories of the New Testament for me, where we tend to consider the stories in the context of the words, instead of the whole social setting and life experience. Take Bartimaeus, for instance. He had also been sighted but at some time had become blind. He asked for the recovery of his sight, and Jesus restored him. At first, he followed Jesus with the crowd, and you can imagine him sharing his story on the way with any who would listen.

At some point, he would have gone home. What was his reception like? Was everyone as overwhelmed with joy as he was? Did some doubt that he had ever been blind in the first place? Was he challenged by doubters amongst his friends or even family?

What was their response when he'd first lost his sight? Did they now feel betrayed? He had earned his maintenance by begging. How was he going to survive now? How did he even recognise his way, his home or his friends and family? By sight or by sound? How easily did he adjust to his new situation, and how did the various members of his network adjust to him?

A year later, Mary and Peter came back unannounced to visit us again on their wedding anniversary. They wanted to thank God for giving them such a gift that evening in the chapel. Her eyes were steady. She admitted that she was having difficulty with some of her peripheral vision, but her main sight was fine.

I asked about the children.

'They really struggled to believe that I could see. They kept on gathering around me and asking questions about the colour of their eyes or what exactly they were doing around the room.'

Joy filled her as she recounted these stories. It seemed to be contagious. Indeed, she and Peter had led many young people to Christ since the miracle.

As we reflect on the works that God does, we can sometimes imagine that He usually uses those who have a high profile in society. But, in reality, He often works through nameless and faceless people, everyday people. If we invite Him, He can work through you and me.

We will consider this further in the next session.

Session 2

BEING BLESSED

Gather with your group. When everyone is comfortable, work through the material below. Go slowly and reflectively. Honour each other's comments. Watch the video at the recommended point, then continue working through the questions together.

Scripture

And afterwards,
    I will pour out my Spirit on all people.
Your sons and daughters will prophesy,
      your old men will dream dreams,
      your young men will see visions.
Even on my servants, both men and women,
      I will pour out my Spirit in those days. (Joel 2:28–29)

Prayer

- **Individual:** Speak out and reflect on the following prayer.
- **Group:** Say this prayer together.

Glory to the Father and to the Son and to the Holy Spirit.
Into Your hands, O Lord, I commend my spirit.
Keep me as the apple of Your eye.
Hide me under the shadow of Your wings.
Save us, O Lord, while we reflect on You, and guard us while
    we talk,
that our awakened hearts may watch with Christ
and our mouths bring peace to the houses, streets, corners and
    wide-open places to which You take us.

We can know the facts of a situation or have an understanding of the doctrine or theology that describes the ministry of Jesus but still not have grasped the emotions at work or the relationships involved. Let us explore how we establish a firm foundation for being a blessing and declaring blessings.

Suggested statement from the group leader: 'One key principle relates to a revelation about the Father heart of God and His love for us. Roy Godwin has some teaching that will help us reflect on this.'

Play Video: SESSION TWO

We encourage you to take notes as you watch the video. Feel free to use the space under the Your Notes header following this paragraph. Note anything that you find especially helpful or provokes you to examine the way you view what it means to love God and follow Jesus in the world today.

Your Notes

Review

What helped or provoked you in what Roy shared in the video? Underline the key points in the notes you made. If you are part of a group, share together, if that would be helpful.

Reflect

Do you have any stories about your own understanding of the Father heart of God and how you discovered this understanding? What Scripture stories, verses or principles have also helped you in this respect? Write them in your notes. If you are part of a group, share together, if that would be helpful.

Focus

- **Individual:** The following Key Insights section provides supporting scriptures and a deeper look into the content of this session to supplement what you have already noted.
- **Group:** If you're studying as a group, your group leader will now summarise some of the things that you have shared together. Be ready to note any additional points he or she may make that could be helpful to you. The following Key Insights section provides supporting scriptures and a deeper look into the content of this session. Use this material to supplement what you have already noted and to aid further discussion. You may find it useful for personal reflection at a later date as well.

Key Insights

1. God desires to engage with us and to reveal His heart and purposes to us.

> In the last days, God says,
>   "I will pour out my Spirit on all people.
> Your sons and daughters will prophesy,
>   your young men will see visions,
>   your old men will dream dreams.
> Even on my servants, both men and women,
>   I will pour out my Spirit in those days,
>   and they will prophesy." (Acts 2:17–18)

> Surely the Sovereign LORD does nothing
>   without revealing his plan
>   to his servants the prophets. (Amos 3:7)

2. God desires our return to relationship and the healing of our damaged emotions.

> So he got up and went to his father.
> But while he was still a long way off, his father saw him and was filled with compassion for him; he ran to his son, threw his arms round him and kissed him. (Luke 15:20)

3. We should beware of false burdens and wrong expectations.

> Take my yoke upon you and learn from me, for I am gentle and humble in heart, and you will find rest for your souls. For my yoke is easy and my burden is light. (Matt. 11:29–30)

4. We stand on the promises of God.

> This is how we know what love is: Jesus Christ laid down his life for us. (1 John 3:16)

> Therefore, there is now no condemnation for those who are in Christ Jesus. (Rom. 8:1)

5. God loves His enemies and desires good things for them.

> You have heard that it was said, 'Love your neighbour and hate your enemy.' But I tell you, love your enemies and pray for those who persecute you, that you may be children of your Father in heaven. He causes his sun to rise on the evil and the good, and sends rain on the righteous and the unrighteous. (Matt. 5:43–45)

Your Notes

Prayer

As we conclude our session, we turn to prayer, talking to the God who blesses and declaring our own blessing and thankfulness towards Him. You can use the following prayer and/or the prayer idea below it.

> Father God, in view of Your great mercy, we lay our lives down
> as a sacrifice for You.
> Choosing to die to self,
> We ask You to pour Your mighty resurrection power through us,
> That Jesus may be revealed and Your kingdom come in power,
> Changing us and redeeming the world.
> Amen.

Prayer Idea

- **Individual:** Read Psalm 103:8–13 through twice. Identify any words or phrases that strike you and stir your heart. Speak out a prayer that reflects your gratitude to God for the truth of the words that spoke to you.
- **Group:** Have one person read Psalm 103:8–13 to the whole group twice through. As the person reads, identify any words or phrases that strike you and stir your heart. When it is time to pray, speak out a prayer that reflects your gratitude to God for the truth of the words that spoke to you.

The LORD is compassionate and gracious,
   slow to anger, abounding in love.
He will not always accuse,
   nor will he harbour his anger for ever;
he does not treat us as our sins deserve
   or repay us according to our iniquities.
For as high as the heavens are above the earth,
   so great is his love for those who fear him;
as far as the east is from the west,
   so far has he removed our transgressions from us.
As a father has compassion on his children,
   so the LORD has compassion on those who fear him.
      (Ps. 103:8–13)

Life Activity

When you get up from this study and before the next session, take this verse as your watchword:

> Are not two sparrows sold for a penny? Yet not one of them will
> fall to the ground outside your *Father's* care. (Matt. 10:29)

As your group dismisses and you all go back to your lives, remember to *look for the Father heart of God in all the situations, places and people that you encounter this week.* Send up an 'arrow' prayer to God, asking Him to reveal His heart in those situations and the people in them. Ask for His *grace* and *revelation* to go before His people, preparing the way for the people of God.

Session 2:
Going
Deeper

BEING BLESSED

Further Material for Personal Reading

Some time ago, a young woman came up to Daphne and me as we were breaking for lunch during one of our monthly Prayer Days. Looking quietly at Daphne, she said that while Daphne had been speaking, one of her ears had popped and she could hear clearly with it. We thanked her for telling us and left for a sandwich. The following day, this woman was in our Morning Prayers and asked at the close whether she could have a quick word with me.

She explained that she had suffered a severe head trauma which had left her deaf in one ear and weak on one side of her body, resulting in her having difficulty with coordination. Suddenly being able to hear again was absolutely wonderful—she had been told that she would never hear in that ear again. The following morning, she wanted to share more with me, this time to say that she was finding herself much stronger and that she could control her weak hand, leg and foot far better. Again, we rejoiced with her, affirmed and blessed her and blessed the work that God was doing in her.

The next day was a glorious blue-sky day and very warm. During Evening Prayers, we felt crowded in the prayer room. So we all went out into the court-yard to get some fresh air. God was very present and there was quite a hubbub as everyone chatted excitedly. The young woman approached me again and asked to have a word.

The chatter ceased as everyone moved closer and listened in. She explained that she had undergone many operations on her head and skull and that noth-ing more could be done for her from a medical standpoint. As well as suffering emotional depression, she also had an actual physical depression on her temple where she had been struck. The surgeon had said that the bone would not grow anymore, and she would carry the wound for the rest of her life.

I gently commiserated, but she carried on. That morning, she had awakened with a sense of heat and tingling across her temple. She had never experienced that previously, and it disturbed her. She had put her hand to her head, but—she looked shocked as she said the words—there was no longer any depression there, just solid bone!

At that point, the eavesdroppers looked as though they were going to join me in overflowing thankfulness and praise. But her next words stopped us in our tracks. 'I can hear again, and I'm hugely improved in strength and coordination. Also, the impossible has happened: the bone has healed across my head. Doesn't matter much though, does it?'

You could have heard a pin drop. Even the birds seemed to silence their songs as they listened, and the breeze held its breath. I felt lost as I asked what she meant.

'Oh,' she said, 'because of the much bigger miracle.'

Intrigued, lost, aware of everyone looking at me and wanting to know what was going to happen next (and feeling quite wary), I again asked what she meant.

She said that God had revealed Himself to her as a caring Father who loved her, affirmed her and accepted her, showing that He wasn't at all the angry, disappointed judge she had always imagined. In that moment, she recognised Him as the Father she had always longed for in her deepest being.

I may have shouted for joy at that point, but again she ignored my response and said there was more. 'More than that?' I asked. Yes, there was.

She explained that when God had revealed His true self to her, He had also revealed who *she* really was. Looking directly at me, she said she knew now that she wasn't the person who people had always said she was, as a worthless member of a rather despised people group. God had revealed to her that in His eyes she was lovely and that she filled Him with joy. It had nothing to do with her looks or her performance—it was just the outpouring of His compassionate, undeserved, unearned, accepting love. She had discovered for herself that God was the Father she always longed for. He's truly amazing in every way.

A new chapter was written in her life that day. It would become part of her backstory.

We each have a backstory, and mine is as mixed up as so many other people's.

Like everyone, I was shaped by my younger life. The environment I was born into, the schools, house moves, bullying and loneliness, all compounded by the attitude of my father, whom I did not remember ever having affirmed me in any way. A whole maelstrom of childhood experience, stretching onwards into my youth, persuaded me that I was totally unlovable and deserved every bad thing I received.

Broken promises and disappointments took away any expectation that good things were available for me. Coupled to that, for much of that time, I wanted to die, mainly because of the pain inflicted on me by a then-untreatable illness.

I was a mess. The uncomfortable truth is that we are (almost) all messed up or see ourselves as victims. Many adults struggle with life because of their childhood experiences with parents and circumstances. It's easy to find someone to blame externally so we can shrug our shoulders and say that we are what we are because of so-and-so. It's not my fault. I cannot help the way I was treated or the circumstances I had to endure. It was *their* fault. Etc.

The world is full of people who would evidence that attitude. But the good news of Jesus Christ really is good news. It involves a new birth, the embracing of a whole new outlook and way of life.

When Jesus died on the cross, he bore not only my sins but also my pains and griefs. 'He was despised and rejected by men, a man of sorrows and acquainted with grief.… Surely he has borne our griefs and carried our sorrows' (Isa. 53:3–4 ESV). They were all nailed to the cross, where He, not I, carried them. Jesus died in my place, carrying my every wound and rejection into the darkness of death. When He arose, He no longer carried them.

He has set me free from victimhood and empowers me to step outside of that real but dead fabric of past pain to taste the power of the resurrection in my life, relationships, attitudes and circumstances.

When we choose to follow Jesus, and make ourselves available to God, He takes all the joy of our past experience and weaves it into His purpose for us. The miracle is that He also takes our woundedness and redeems that too. He shapes our character and turns us into servants of the living God in place of being sinful, failed and wounded beings.

It's time to forgive … to list those who we believe have robbed or wounded us and forgive them. I have often found that to be quite a struggle, but once we tell God that we can't do it on our own and need His help, it becomes far easier.

And to repent … which is to turn away from old ways and attitudes and head in a new direction. *I'm not a victim; because of Jesus, I'm a conqueror.* I'm open and responsible for new attitudes and fresh goals. I accept responsibility for my life—and for my attitudes.

To be a Christian is to accept radical personal change that causes me to become personally accountable for my own attitudes and my lifestyle. God is constantly drawing us into ongoing change. As someone said, 'God loves us too much to leave us as we are.'

Paul describes how we are being transformed from one degree of glory to another as we look at Jesus (see 2 Cor. 3:18). A degree is such a tiny measurement, but it's all about step-by-step change. A child may say, 'You made me as I am,' but an adult says, 'By the grace of God, I am being made new.'

The idea of blessing others also has a biblical backstory, and it's rooted in the Father heart of God.

Jesus came to reveal the heavenly Father, breaking open the religious and Jewish cultural boxes to let Him out. He is Abba, Daddy. He broke the lies and traditions that held people in dark captivity, because the Father desperately wants to be revealed, to be found. All along, He has been present in our loneliness, pain and grief.

I'm not a victim; because of Jesus, I'm a conqueror.

In times of sin or rebellion, He has been the patient, longing Father waiting to run and greet us at the slightest sign of our looking towards Him. He grieves over our blindness and the lies, caricatures and deceits that have distorted our understanding of who He is. We only have to take a step, and He comes running to grab us, hug us and weep over us. He is a Father who has been grieving over our absence and is inconsolable until we return (see Luke 15:20).

As we take hold of the idea that we can and should pronounce blessing for people and communities, our passion for others will be provoked by the character of God exhibited in Jesus.

Being Released from False Burdens and Wrong Expectations

What does God expect of us? I am privileged to spend time with many Christian leaders. Very often, they voice frustration and disappointment with their lives and their ministries. They frequently (but not always) find themselves battling to satisfy the demands of God, their own concepts of what it means to be good or successful leaders and the expectations of their congregations.

No wonder they often struggle with insecurity and a sense of inferiority or are heading towards burnout. Most times, the choice appears to be between disguising their inner torment and carrying on as if on a treadmill, one step at a time, becoming acutely depressed on the way or throwing themselves into manic activity.

At those and similar moments in all of our lives, we might hear Jesus saying the uncomfortable words to us, 'Woe to you, because you load people down with burdens they can hardly carry' (Luke 11:46). God wants to release you from false burdens and wrong expectations. Let me describe how that once happened for me.

It was a normal-looking Prayer Day. One day each month, we used to meet for several hours to worship, pray, encourage one another, share testimony, read the Word together and have opportunity for ministry. People were sometimes travelling one hundred miles to join with us for just a few hours, which seemed amazing. But when I asked how far people had come on this particular morning, I was hearing that some had travelled an impossible one, two, three, and even eleven thousand miles! We had attendees from North America, Europe, Africa, Asia, Australia, New Zealand and beyond.

My impulse was to cry out to God and ask Him to help me deliver something so wonderful that it would justify their time and money in getting to us. I had fallen straight into the trap of performance and expectation that I placed upon myself, and it was a heavy burden. Unfortunately, I stayed in the trap for some time.

We started to worship, and contrary to our usual experience, there was no flow, no sense of life. It was muted, to say the least. The team cast anxious looks towards me and I to them. At the lunch break, we wondered together what was wrong. We cried out for help and expected that the worship would really flow when we restarted.

It didn't. What was worse: I didn't feel that the word I was bringing was equal to the congregation, and I wanted something new to really inspire them. It didn't come. By the time we got to the end, all I could think of was escape. I was embarrassed, angry with God, wondering what was going on.

Yet the moment we closed, people started rushing forward, wanting to say how thrilled they were with the worship, the like of which they had never known, and how impacted they were by the word. Some of them even testified to being healed of hurts and pain as they listened.

I slipped away in considerable confusion and frustration, and as soon as I could, I got alone with the Lord. I asked Him to show me what was going on, and to my surprise, He was awaiting me and ready to respond at that very moment.

In my mind, I saw a large banqueting table laid out with scores of places prepared and set. Then He explained that I had a choice. If I wanted to determine what the menu should be, the size of portions and so on, I could do so.

On the other hand, He knew every person who would be seated there; He knew their needs and capacity and the food and portion that were perfectly suited to each one. Some could cope with a small cool dish; others were ready for a very large roast meat meal. In that scenario, He would prepare the food and I could be the waiter who carried no weight of responsibility but who simply served what the master chef had prepared. Which role did I prefer?

It didn't take a nanosecond to decide. From that moment, all thoughts of performance for acceptance were vanquished. I had been set free.

Nowadays, I may be speaking to a small congregation or to a gathering of thousands, or on live TV, but I am still relaxed. All I will do is deliver the dish that the Father has prepared. What happens next is up to Him, not to me. I am secure in my heavenly Father's love; I am fully known and fully accepted. I have nothing to prove and no approval to win. My Father's verdict is that I am His son whom He loves and in whom He is well pleased. It's an outrageous affirmation from an outrageous God.

Provoking Your Spiritual Imagination

One of my early memories is of standing in the pulpit and praying, reading the Scriptures and preaching my eight-year-old heart out in the Baptist church which my parents helped found, while my mother was busy cleaning the building. Everyone knew that one day I would be a missionary. It was all I dreamt of until I was into my teens.

Then, when I could drive, I joined a church plant on a nearby American airbase. The pastor, Malcolm Baker, a very direct Welshman, graciously and generously mentored me and some other young men. Later, I would go to Bible college, where amongst other things I did research into the revival history of Wales, Ireland and the USA. My *redeemed* backstory, my expectation of what God might do in and through me, was being formed.

It was at this time that I came across a biography of John Sung, and this affected me in a more practical way. John Sung had a relatively short ministry, mostly during the 1930s. He was a brilliant Chinese academic who as a young man went to North America to obtain a doctorate in physics. His father was a pastor, and John had been converted as a child through a breath of revival that reached China at a time in connection with the revival in Wales.

Back again in China, John commenced an extremely effective ministry amongst students. He joined the Bethel Worldwide Evangelistic Band, a missions grouping led then by Andrew Gih which was evangelising far and wide. John was in many ways unique. He had some idiosyncratic views of the Bible and of preaching. He could be very theatrical, sometimes balancing on the communion rail as he preached, and he was firmly opposed to Western Pentecostalism.

Then God seemed to grasp John in a new way. He had a totally unexpected personal experience of the Holy Spirit, and he became a man with a mission and a man on fire. He remained biblically orthodox and now expected God to move in power, confirming the Word with signs following. He would preach the gospel, heal the sick and where necessary set people free from bondage. Time was short; war was stirring in the region.

In only a few years, it is estimated that 100,000 people surrendered to the Lord through John Sung's missions. His ministry was so effective that it is said that anyone in Southeast Asia today who is a third-generation Christian probably has John Sung somewhere in the family story.

For example, whilst in Southeast Asia a short while ago, I was chatting with a pastor who told me that he was a third-generation Christian. Apparently, his grandmother had been a terror to Christians, actually chasing them out of the house if they dared come near her. She was blind and a vehement hater of Christianity.

One day, some friends persuaded her to go with them to a John Sung meeting attended by thousands. When he walked into the packed church, he went straight across to her and laid hands on her—she received her sight and immediately gave her life to the Lord. Now here was her grandson, a third-generation Christian, leading others to the Lord.

As I read the stories in John's biography, I found myself profoundly stirred in my spirit. This was how I wanted to minister, in step with the Holy Spirit. I wanted to see Him confirm the Word with signs following in my own ministry. I didn't want to be John Sung; I wanted to be Roy Godwin but with John Sung's God in my life.

That was good, because that was who God had planned for me to be as well. And He wants you to be—you! And when we bless people, it's that they may mature into their own fullness of life in Jesus.

Shortly after praying in this way, I too was radically changed through an unexpected encounter with the Holy Spirit, who turned my life upside down. Immediately, I began to see exceptional fruit. I would pray for sick people, and in the main they would be healed; hundreds responded to the gospel invitation, particularly young people. It was a very heady time. Astonishingly, our cooperation with God brings the Father joy.

We cannot compare our experience with someone else's ministry. You and I have not received their calling or ministry. Ours is not likely to be as dramatic a life as for some—it isn't a competition, thank God. So why do we feel that it is? We are each unique, working out our discipleship in the context of our personal world, life and circumstances. We must be faithful only with what is entrusted to us, whatever the measure.

It is a wonderful truth that you and I bring the Father joy; but it is not your ministry, your performance as a disciple with its ups and downs, that He is most thrilled with. No, what thrills Him most is—you yourself!

The Father's Joy

When Jesus was baptised in the Jordan by John the Baptist, the Father couldn't hold back His joy. Breaking through the realm of eternity into our world of time and space, He thundered forth with, 'This is my Son, whom I love; with him I am well pleased' (Matt. 3:17). Mark's gospel remembers it as being slightly more personalised: 'You are my Son, whom I love; with you I am well pleased' (Mark 1:11). The New Living Translation says, 'You are my dearly loved Son, and you bring me great joy.'

What a statement! What affection. What joy. What affirmation. As a youngster, and even as a young man, I longed to feel loved, affirmed. There was a gaping hole in my heart, in my emotions, and it never got easier. For years, I battled against suicidal desires.

'You are my Son,' said the Father to Jesus in front of the crowds. A public affirmation with fatherly delight—that's settled then. What acknowledgement before men; what security! But well pleased, joyful? Jesus hadn't done anything yet; His ministry hadn't begun. The approval was totally disconnected from His performance. So, when His ministry did commence, He had nothing to prove because He had already been totally accepted, acknowledged and approved before He'd even started. This was important. He obeyed the Father's will and purpose out of a love relationship, not out of a desire to win His Father's love by performing well.

In stark contrast, I had felt so unloved and unlovable that I found myself trapped in a permanent desire to perform so desperately well in every way so that someone, somewhere might love and approve of me.

As I looked at those verses then, and as I look at them now, I remember that I too am a child of God. My heavenly Father has personally chosen me—and He's not disappointed, even when I disappoint myself and everyone else. How can that be? He is love, mercy and grace wrapped up in endless support and patience towards me. He knows how frail I am, how weak, yet He endlessly takes me as I am. Instead of nasty retorts when I stumble or fail to meet some genuine or imagined demand, He is there to speedily help me up, dust me down and assist me to start again.

Merciful, merciful, merciful is my Father. He is the only One who can meet my deepest needs, and most amazingly, He longs to do so. When I don't want to look in the mirror, He gazes at my face with such overwhelming compassion and still more acceptance, clothed in joy. When others speak ill of me, He speaks well of me. When the enemy attacks, He helps me to stand. Such grace! He is not ashamed to be known as my Father or to own me as His child.

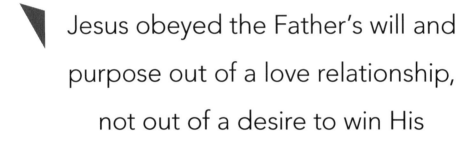

Jesus obeyed the Father's will and purpose out of a love relationship, not out of a desire to win His Father's love by performing well.

Jesus says that when we are weary and heavy-laden, we can come to Him for rest. His yoke is easy, and His burden is light. When I was young, I wondered about the weights that I carried in contrast to those words and realised that they were a big, mixed bundle. There were my insecurities, the weight of painful words that were said by my father. There were all the stresses of trying to present myself as a whole person when I was so broken inside.

Then there were the weights of expectation always crushing me.

Some were unachievable, such as those of my father, but then there were the demands of my heavenly Father, of Christian leaders, of 'churchianity's' religious culture. There were the condemnations of my own heart as well as of the enemy. As for my sins, my failures … What about my disappointments, and the knowledge that I so easily disappointed others around me as well as those dearest to me?

Come to Me and find rest (see Matt. 11:28).

Then I sensed the Father's outrageous love and acceptance of me, even of me, who has been made by grace a child of God. My performance was not the measuring rod of my life; the price He was willing to pay that He might have me, a price paid long before I could have pleased Him or sought to influence Him, has become the standard. The cross is His affirmation of me personally, of my value to Him, of my worth. On Calvary's hill, He publicly owned, loved and valued me.

And not only me but all of humanity. This is how we know what love is (see 1 John 3:16). There is therefore no more condemnation for those who follow Him; no, neither is there a demand for performance to earn His love (see Rom. 8:1).

To see people's physical ears or eyes opened through the mighty name of Jesus is a wondrous thing, and we rejoice with great joy when we see it. But what happens with greater frequency is that God breaks through into someone's understanding of who He is and there is an immediate change of relationship. Sometimes this has happened through the sharing of the Word, but very often it has been through sovereign revelation.

I have found myself growing in the experiences I had always longed for. Not only did I know the truth, but I was walking in it, which is when it sets you free (see John 8:32).

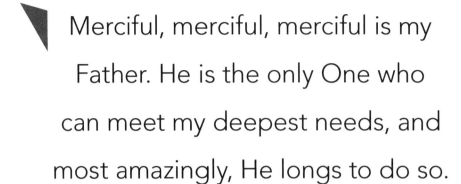

Merciful, merciful, merciful is my Father. He is the only One who can meet my deepest needs, and most amazingly, He longs to do so.

A wonderful bishop friend of ours expressed it so clearly: 'This is how the kingdom works. When you know you are loved, you find yourself loving others. When you know you are forgiven, you find yourself forgiving others. When you find yourself accepted, you find yourself accepting others.' There is an outflow, a reflection of what He has done for you, towards others as your heart attitudes change. So of course, aware of having received such undeserved blessing, you want to share more about the kindness, love and compassion of God by blessing others.

That is God's calling for you: to know Him and to serve His purpose by releasing blessings to others, as we will see in the next session.

CALLED TO BLESS

Gather with your group. When everyone is comfortable, work through the material below. Go slowly and reflectively. Honour each other's comments. Watch the video at the recommended point, then continue working through the questions together.

Scripture

When you enter a house, first say, 'Peace to this house.' (Luke 10:5)

Prayer

- **Individual:** Speak the following prayer aloud, slowly and reflectively.
- **Group:** Say the following prayer together, slowly and reflectively.

Christ as a light, illumine and guide me.

Christ as a shield, overshadow me.

Christ under me,

Christ over me,

Christ beside me, on my left and my right.

This day, be within and without me,

Lowly and meek, yet all-powerful.

Be in the heart of each to whom I speak,

In the mouth of each who speaks unto me.

This day, be within and without me,

Lowly and meek, yet all-powerful.

Christ as a light,

Christ as a shield,

Christ beside me on my left and my right.

(Excerpt from St. Patrick's Breastplate)

Suggested statement from the group leader: 'How do we respond to our calling as those who are to be God's agents of blessing in the world? What encouragements and challenges does this bring to us and our understanding of the sacred at work in everyday life? Roy Godwin has some teaching that will help us reflect on this.'

Play Video: SESSION THREE

We encourage you to take notes as you watch the video. Feel free to use the space under the Your Notes header following this paragraph. Note anything that you find especially helpful or provokes you to examine the way you view what it means to love God and to follow Jesus in the world today.

Your Notes

Review

What helped or provoked you in what Roy shared in the video? Underline the key points in the notes you made. If you are part of a group, share together, if that would be helpful.

Reflect

Do you have any additional insights that you have gained about our role in the mission of God in the world? What Scripture stories, verses or principles spring to your mind as you reflect on this topic? Can you think of any stories of blessing others that would root this in everyday life today? Write them in your notes. If you are part of a group, share them, if that would be helpful.

Focus

- **Individual:** The following Key Insights section provides supporting scriptures and a deeper look into the content of this session to supplement what you have already noted.

- **Group:** If you're studying as a group, your group leader will now summarise some of the things that you have shared together. Be ready to note any additional points he or she may make that could be helpful to you. The following Key Insights section provides supporting scriptures and a deeper look into the content of this session. Use this material to supplement what you have already noted and to aid further discussion. You may find it useful for personal reflection at a later date as well.

Key Insights

1. Scripture reveals a pattern.

God spoke blessing as He created the earth, and Scripture soon established a pattern of parents blessing their children.

Then in the book of Numbers, we find God commissioning Aaron to declare His blessing over the people (see Num. 6:22–27; Lev. 9:22–24). Roy mentioned these passages in the video, but you might want to read them aloud.

2. The Holy Spirit accompanies us.

We are not alone in this work—the Holy Spirit goes before us, preparing hearts. The call to us is to be available to participate in what God is doing. The Holy Spirit provokes people towards understanding of what they see of God unfolding before them.

3. The life of Jesus shows us the way.

We have an example. Jesus is a role model for the everyday encounters of life. The gospel is first encountered by people in many different ways.

Jesus says:

- To the blind—receive your sight.
- To the paralysed—rise up and walk. (And by the way, your sins are forgiven.)
- To the deaf—hear.
- To the feverish—be released.
- To the unclean—you are cleansed.
- To the dead—rise up.
- To the demonised—be set free.
- To the sinful—your sins are forgiven.
- To the outsider who doesn't belong and has no place—you are welcome.

We too have that calling to bless people so that the goodness of God might be at work in their lives.

4. Worship helps us know God.

As we worship, we are drawn into reflection on the character of God and His work in the world. We become immersed in who He is. Being a person of blessing requires more from us than words spoken. God calls us to live lives of blessing. Values-based discipleship nurtures every part of our being so that being a blessing can become who we are.

The prophet and the psalmist hold out a promise to us: 'Direct me in the path of your commands, for there I find delight' (Ps. 119:35).

Worship helps us develop instructed tongues that say the words that can sustain the weary (see Isa. 50:4). We are equipped for our calling. Just as the Levites were called both to stand in His presence and to declare His presence, we too can be carriers of the blessing to our communities (see Deut. 10:8; 21:5).

5. The prayers of the kingdom echo our calling.

The Lord's Prayer is a faith framework that helps us understand our calling in the world. It reminds us of our new relationship with God, requests that God show His character (His holiness) to the world and asks for the coming of the kingdom of heaven to earth. It reminds us to forgive as we have been forgiven, and it asks for God's supply during times of trial or shortage.

6. We are to become a kingdom of priests.

This call to blessing is not the task of a select few. It is an opportunity for all who believe in the name of Jesus. God tells His people that they will be a kingdom of priests, and Peter reminds the followers of Jesus that this calling is also upon them (Ex. 19:5-6; 1 Pet. 2:5, 9–10).

7. We can bring life to others.

Christians are not mere purveyors of ideas; we are also bringers of life. There is a joy to be found that is like when Jesus was 'full of joy in the Holy Spirit' as the disciples returned from praying, working, declaring, healing and sharing about the kingdom (Luke 10).

God wants to reconcile all things to Himself by equipping us to be carriers of His love (Col. 1:20). Being a people of blessing is like a tapestry of rich colours where different threads and patterns from the life of Jesus and the Bible story come together to paint a beautiful picture of God's desire for us.

Your Notes

Prayer

As we conclude our session, we turn to prayer, seeking the empowerment of the Holy Spirit as we go from here to fulfil our calling to bless the communities in which we find ourselves. You can use the following prayer and/or the prayer idea outlined below it.

> Bless us now, Lord, as we go from here;
> Be with us and all who are dear to us.
> Be in the eye of all who see us;
> In the mouth of all who speak with us.

Keep us in the beautiful attitudes,
Joyful, simple and gentle.

May the favour of the Lord our God rest on us;
   establish the work of our hands for us—
   yes, establish the work of our hands. (Ps. 90:17)

Amen.

Prayer Idea

Take a moment for quiet reflection. Think about one place outside your home where you go fairly frequently. It can be anywhere—school, shop, workplace, gym etc.

- **Individual:** As you pray, ask for the empowerment of God for wisdom, compassion and proclamations of blessing for that place. Seek His heart for that place, and make note of what was prompted in your mind. In the next session, we will dig a little deeper on how to respond to that prompting.
- **Group:** As the group joins together in public prayer, ask for the empowerment of God for wisdom, compassion and proclamations of blessing for that place. Seek His heart for that place, and make note of what was prompted in your mind. In the next session, we will dig a little deeper on how to respond to that prompting.

Life Activity

When you get up from this study and before the next session, take this verse as your watchword:

> Moses and Aaron then went into the tent of meeting. When they came out, they blessed the people; and the glory of the LORD appeared to all the people. (Lev. 9:23)

As your group dismisses and you all go back to your everyday tasks, ask God to remind you of an aspect of His life, beauty, creativity and generosity that He desires to reveal for those situations. Send up an 'arrow' prayer to God, asking Him for wisdom as you bring blessing in words, deeds and commitment to that community.

Session 3:
Going
Deeper

CALLED TO BLESS
Further Material for Personal Reading

What is the purpose of our lives? We don't get a practice run. This is it. Since we live only once, and because the older you get the faster it seems to go, doesn't it make sense to live the best and most purposeful life that we possibly can? Someone once said that *the way to live the fullest life is to understand what God is doing in the world today and throw yourself into it.* Here's a very extreme modern-day example of just that.

D radiated beauty as she spoke with us at a small gathering of Christians in a tent on the grounds of a magnificent Welsh castle. We couldn't understand a word she said—she spoke no English—but fortunately, a translator from an English university had been persuaded to help.

She was explaining how new believers were taught to follow Jesus in her area of China. She told us that they would be taken to a network of caves on a remote cliff face, where they would learn from ordinary Chinese Christians who had been following Jesus for some time. It was a dangerous thing to do, for the teachers and the new disciples alike. If found, they would be beaten and imprisoned, or worse.

Their first lesson in discipleship was … how to take a beating!

Jesus took a beating from the Roman soldiers. Paul knew beatings, whipping, stoning, imprisonment and shipwrecks. Jesus promised that those who followed Him would be very blessed … and persecuted.

Someone asked D whether she had personally known suffering for Christ. Reluctantly, she pulled back her hair from one side of her face, and we saw a terrible scar. That was the result of being beaten with a prison keyring. She then showed us her twisted fingers from the torture she had endured, including having her fingernails torn out many times.

Another person asked how many people she had led to faith in Jesus, and her quiet answer shocked the translator. He double-checked with her, but she insisted that he had heard correctly. An elderly Chinese man travelling with her confirmed it. The network for which she was responsible numbered some three million people!

It blew our minds. We looked at her, this diminutive figure of whom we had never heard, with awe and respect. A tiny 'unknown' apostle of Christ with a mighty God and a staggering ministry. The beauty she radiated was the beauty of Jesus, refined by her sufferings. D knew exactly what her purpose in life was, and she was living it to the full.

Several years later, I was filming on the subject of revival with a group of underground Chinese leaders. Not only had they heard of D, but they also knew her well. They assured me that her network had grown much larger, as hundreds of thousands more continued to come to faith.

When Jesus called the first disciples to follow Him, they entered a new life and a new future. It was a radical and stimulating time as they listened and observed their Master. They had intimate time with the Lamb of God and got to know Him. It got tougher, though, when each one discovered that he was just flesh, as were the other eleven, and that they had to learn to live together. Some things had to change!

It was exciting when they saw astonishing miracles with healings and deliverance alongside forgiveness of sin and calls to repentance. Crowds thronged around Jesus, and He taught them about the kingdom of God. In private, they discussed together the meaning of the parables that He spoke. His teachings seemed out of this world. They marvelled at His wisdom in dealing with those who opposed Him and how He broke the boundaries to show acceptance and value to others.

Then came the day when Jesus told the twelve they were going on a journey. No, not with Him at their side. This time, they would be going in pairs, and they were to take nothing with them but the clothes they wore. No spares, no money, no walking aids, nothing but reliance on their heavenly Father's provision, just as Jesus constantly demonstrated every day. Having closely observed Jesus, they were now being sent to imitate His life and ministry before others.

Jesus delegated His mandate to them, and it became their own. He appointed power and authority to the twelve, equipping them to do the job. They were to carry God's blessing into each community. To speak peace into the houses that were open to them, calling for peace to rest on the home. To seek the good of the community, to announce the kingdom of God, and to heal the sick. Imitating Jesus, they were to speak His words and do His deeds with His authority and power.

I find it hard to believe that they greeted this news with great excitement. Fear seems more likely, and a desire to run away. I can imagine their panicked reasoning: maybe a few more years of observing Jesus would be better first, slowly giving them more confidence. Then perhaps they could begin to explore in a small way whether such a ministry might be viable for them or not. After all, people are all different, aren't they? But no, Jesus said, 'Go! Right now!' He promised them that His Father would supply all their needs as they sought His kingdom and His righteousness first (see Matt. 6:33–34).

To follow Jesus involves repentance and forgiveness, entering into the love of God and enjoying Him. It involves transformation, our character being moulded and shaped as we are changed from one degree of glory to another. It is a call into community—we are grafted into the family of God. Yet God's purpose for us is greater than this alone. When we believe, we are commissioned to begin speaking the words of Jesus and doing the works and wonders of Jesus wherever we are. We are called into God's mission to bear witness to the world.

What is our purpose in life? As Christians, our purpose is to fully enter into all that Jesus has won for us, to fellowship with the Holy Spirit, to enjoy the love of our heavenly Father and to serve His purposes on earth, invoking the power of the age to come and releasing His blessing into a needy world.

In the Beginning …

When God created the world, He did so by speaking a word. Hebrews 1 says that in these last days He has spoken to us through His Son. Jesus said that His sheep recognised His voice.

Our God is a speaking God, unlike the other pretender gods we manufacture for ourselves. And He speaks blessing from the very beginning. When we read the story of creation, we see that the first thing God did when He created men and women was to bless them. Later, He made promises of blessing to Abraham. In fact, He tied the concept of blessing into future history, 'His story': 'All peoples on earth will be blessed through you' (Gen. 12:3).

The Father has always longed to pour blessings out upon all flesh.

You and I are inheritors of the blessings of Abraham. We have received the blessing of the news of the sacrificial death of our Saviour and have believed. Now, His Spirit is in us as a deposit of all that is to come in the fullness of time. We carry news of great blessing, and we are called to express it.

Notice that God *said* these things to Abraham. Fundamentally, blessing is spoken word. We might receive a gift and express our gratitude for it by writing a note to say how blessed we were. However, if we were to take an infant to a church service for a blessing, we wouldn't expect to receive a greeting card saying, 'Welcome to this world; have a good life!' We would expect words of significance to be spoken aloud in Jesus' name.

When we speak out blessings, saying the words aloud, we are imitating God. The Holy Spirit then confirms those words. At that moment, Creation's redemption is underway and the lion roars again.

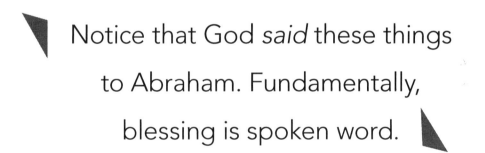

Notice that God *said* these things to Abraham. Fundamentally, blessing is spoken word.

A Kingdom of Priests

You and I have received a high calling, privilege and responsibility: to become priests of God. Peter writes about it in 1 Peter 2:5, 9, saying:

> You also, like living stones, are being built into a spiritual house to be a holy priesthood, offering spiritual sacrifices acceptable to God through Jesus Christ....
>
> You are a chosen people, a royal priesthood, a holy nation, God's special possession, that you may declare the praises of him who called you out of darkness into his wonderful light.

Unfortunately, we can so easily be tangled up by the English term *priesthood*. It sounds suspiciously like clericalism and vocational callings. Maybe historical stories of abuse come to mind in today's world. Surely Peter isn't saying that we should all join the ranks of clergy.

No, he isn't. Peter isn't talking about church leadership or government or unique callings of the few. He is referring to Old Testament prophetic words like Exodus 19:5–6: 'Now if you obey me fully and keep my covenant, then out of all nations you will be my treasured possession. Although the whole earth is mine, you will be for me a kingdom of priests and a holy nation.' Peter is saying, 'This is it! This is who every one of you has become by the grace of our Lord Jesus Christ.'

This is an every-person spiritual priesthood, not an ecclesiastic one—a truth that the Church forgot over the centuries.

Five hundred years ago, there was turmoil in Europe which affected the Church. Martin Luther, a Catholic monk, started confronting the Catholic Church over its corruption and profiteering, particularly regarding its false teaching of salvation by works. He had read the Bible (quite a rare thing in those days, even for clerics) and discovered that salvation came through faith in the Crucified One. This led to what Europeans called the Reformation, the reform of abuses in the Roman Church, leading to the establishment of the Reformed and Protestant Churches.

These three key 'pillars' of belief were established during the Reformation:

- Salvation is by grace alone.
- Ultimate authority is found in the Scriptures alone.
- The priesthood of all believers.

Notice that *priesthood* carries a lowercase *p*. A believer needs no intermediary between him or her and the Father besides Jesus. We have no need of a specialist to speak to God on our behalf. Through Jesus Christ, who has opened a new and living way, we each have direct access for ourselves. This is the priesthood Peter is writing about. Also, this statement recognises that the work of ministry is the work of the believers, the spiritual priesthood, not just a special group of professionals. The apostles, prophets, evangelists, shepherds and teachers are all given to *equip the saints* for the work of ministry (see Eph. 4:12).

A significant part of our work as priests is speaking out words of blessing. It is not reserved for the few. It is the work of every one of us.

We might be used to thinking erroneously that blessing, like all ministries, is reserved for the clergy, particularly if we belong to an episcopal church. It's *their* job to bless. Yes, blessing is a priestly activity, but every Christian is part of a priestly people.

The Catholic Church, an episcopal body, states in its Catechism that 'every baptized person is called to be a "blessing," and to bless.' Even in its services of blessing, 'lay people may preside … [but] the more a blessing concerns ecclesial and sacramental life, the more is its administration reserved to the ordained ministry (bishops, priests, or deacons).'[1] This is helpful in clarifying the distinction between the priesthood of the church and the priesthood of all believers.

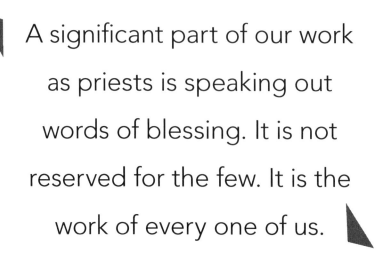

A significant part of our work as priests is speaking out words of blessing. It is not reserved for the few. It is the work of every one of us.

When Jesus says we are to bless those who curse us (Luke 6:28), He is commanding us to be people who speak blessing to others. We find it repeated in Romans 12:14, this time to every disciple in Rome who will read or hear the letter.

A Change of Heart

It is sometimes hard to orient ourselves towards blessing. We view the world around us through a lens of suspicion.

One day, a man knocked on our door and said (in brief), 'I've just got to thank you for changing our lives. This teaching about blessing has changed everything for us. We are so busy blessing everyone that we haven't got time to curse them, which is how we used to live.'

Sadly, that is true for a lot of us. We're against things. As Christians, we are against this and against that. It absolutely amazes me, the number of Christians who are quick to condemn sin in a world of sinners and demand the judgement of God in retaliation.

Have we forgotten that the right time for God to send Jesus into the world for you and me was precisely when you and I were lost in our trespasses and sin? The whole meaning of the doctrine of grace is that God has chosen, and is still choosing, to treat sinners like you and me with favour, though we will never, ever be able to earn it or deserve it. Jesus said that 'those who are well have no need of a physician, but those who are sick.... I came not to call the righteous, but sinners' (Matt. 9:12–13 ESV).

Surely, isn't sin what sinners do, by definition? God has already done something about it by sending Jesus, so He's already acted for them. What's His desire? Is it to swing the axe or pour out the fire of judgement? When the disciples talked like that, Jesus reminded them that this was not His way (Luke 9:54–55). He longed to gather them under His wings. Remember the prodigal son's father? Wafting away the stink of the pigs as he welcomed his son home? Should we not imitate our Lord?

At times, we hear from Christians who believe that we should not speak blessing for people who are not yet Christians. In their view, sinners deserve judgement; or at least everything should go wrong for them with the hope that, in their desperation, they will call on the name of the Lord as a last resort.

The problem with this perspective is that it is simply not reflective of scriptural truth. As we have just seen, the shocking command to bless those who curse you was spoken by Jesus and echoed by Paul.

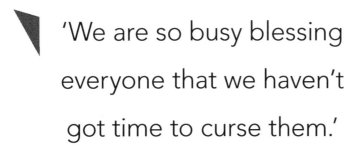

'We are so busy blessing everyone that we haven't got time to curse them.'

The prophet Jeremiah must have sent a shudder through the exiles when he commended them to seek the prosperity of the foreign place where they lived in captivity. They wanted to be back in the holy city of Jerusalem, and here he was telling them to bring blessing to a heathen city (Jer. 29:7). The question is: *Are we going to strut in judgement or walk in grace? Are we going to bless or curse?*

Jesus was profoundly orientated to blessing. Not only did He tell His followers that they were to bless those who cursed them, but He also rebuked His disciples for attempting to block the parents who brought their children to be blessed. This was not an unusual request, and Jesus desired to bless them. The language in the passage about Jesus' embrace of the child conveys the language of adoption. The blessing Jesus gave and His embrace of the child signified the adoption of the child by God and all the mercy, grace, love and favour that this implied (see Mark 10:16).

Jesus reminded His followers that blessing comes to those who give love to the least, the last and the lost. 'But when you give a banquet, invite the poor, the crippled, the lame, the blind, and you will be blessed. Although they cannot repay you, you will be repaid at the resurrection of the righteous' (Luke 14:13–14).

And then Jesus talked of a blessing of power to bear witness: '"I am going to send you what my Father has promised; but stay in the city until you have been clothed with power from on high." When he had led them out to the vicinity of Bethany, he lifted up his hands and blessed them' (Luke 24:49–50). What is the significance of that action? The priests would form a shape with their fingers that symbolised YHWH, the Hebrew name for God. Symbolically, the name of the Lord and all the promise of His character are being placed on the disciples.

Notice that it was whilst He was blessing them that He left them and was taken up into heaven (Luke 24:51). Tongues of fire would later descend in the upper room and empower the disciples for service (Acts 2:3–4).

This was not the first time the blessing of God had been marked by fire:

> Moses and Aaron then went into the tent of meeting. When they came out, they blessed the people; and the glory of the LORD appeared to all the people. Fire came out from the presence of the LORD and consumed the burnt offering and the fat portions on the altar. And when all the people saw it, they shouted for joy and fell face down. (Lev. 9:23–24)

Jesus is our example. He limited His majesty to walk amongst us (Phil. 2:6–7). His humanity and divinity were held together in a way we can barely comprehend. But in His humanity, He ministered and did what He saw the Father doing, and He told the disciples that they could expect to minister in the same way and that they would see even greater things.

In the epic prophecy of Isaiah 61, which Jesus used to announce His ministry, we are told that those who mourn will themselves become ministers of God, priests of the Lord. Jesus used the chapter as His manifesto for ministry. Unlike political manifestos, however, this one was perfectly kept and perfectly enacted.

If we limit our understanding there, though, we make a big mistake. It's now become *our* manifesto, manifested and then delegated to us by Jesus. It is the manifesto of all ministries in the kingdom of God; it's the pattern for ministry by all His servants. All of this is in the context of everything that this passage says about blessing, increase, safety and the flourishing of life.

Elsewhere, the psalmist railed against the enemies of God and mentioned blessing as if it were a commonplace occurrence: 'May those who pass by not say to them, "The blessing of the LORD be on you; we bless you in the name of the LORD"' (Ps. 129:8).

Blessing motifs were deeply woven into the fabric of life in biblical culture. They may have descended into little more than pleasant greetings, but they were rooted in the historic reality of the power of God to bless.

The peace greeting ('Shalom') was part of the social discourse of Jesus' day amongst the people—it was as if you were requesting God's best for the one you greeted. Jesus did not negate that tradition but redeemed it, breathing new life into it and infusing it with the power of God. Powerful, anointed blessing was being released and multiplied on earth.

The practical outworking of your priestly calling is summarised for all the people of God, including you and me, as follows, in Deuteronomy 10:8:

- To carry the ark of the covenant, representing the presence of God
- To stand (without running or rushing) and minister to the Lord
- To speak blessings in His name

Jesus took up this pattern in His ministry. He *stood* in the presence of God through His own drawing aside to pray, noted six times in the book of Luke alone (e.g., 6:12), and His participation in the synagogue and temple patterns of prayer.

Jesus commissioned the seventy-two disciples to minister in the power of the Spirit, and after His resurrection, He breathed on them and blessed them that the peace of God might be with them (John 20:22). They would *carry* His presence.

He provoked them towards blessing by His own resolute commitment to it and His inclusion of it in the instruction to *speak* peace over the households of the towns He sent them to (Luke 10:5). He instructed them to proclaim as they went, *saying aloud*, 'The kingdom of heaven has come near' (Matt. 10:7).

We are released to the full purpose for which we were made when we carry God's presence, minister to Him in spirit and truth and speak blessings. The power and authority for healing and restoration is released when we speak the words that heaven speaks. When we ask that it might be on earth as it is heaven, we are speaking the words that heaven spoke through Jesus.

The miracles that occur can be life-changing.

Kingdom Blessing Demonstrated

With that in mind, we need to be aware that Jesus came to release a new way of living. He came to show us how it is possible to live a godly life while still in human form. Equipped with the anointing of the Holy Spirit and full of the Word of God, we encounter a new life with a power that is rooted in God. We can be in the world but not of the world.

One of the things Jesus came to do was model ministry. He invites us to step into the kingdom now, becoming carriers of the kingdom to others.

We don't go alone, though. The book of Joel reminds us that God will pour out His Spirit on all people (Joel 2:28). It doesn't say the Spirit will come upon merely His followers. It is liberally poured out. It's just that many amongst the *all people* have not yet realised it, or else they have turned their faces away. The implication, however, is that the Holy Spirit is going before us, working in lives and circumstances, even when people have not yet come to understand or see His hand. Dreams and visions are being planted in hearts.

How does this new life work itself out in the nitty-gritty of life? It's easy to conclude a conversation with 'God bless.' It's also easy to say, 'May I bless you?' or 'May I speak a blessing over you (or your life, health, marriage, home, kids, circumstances)?' When we meet the sick, we have the possibility of saying, 'I have good news for you. Would you like to be set free? I set you free in the name of Jesus.' That is the bringing of the gospel—the good news—to that person. We can speak blessings in Jesus' name to individuals, families, communities, regions and nations and physical ground.

When we meet the lonely person who feels cut off and unwelcome, and we say to them, 'Come in, join us,' this brings the kingdom of God near to them. When we meet the demonised person (don't always be looking for demons, by the way—but if they manifest, you do carry the authority to deal with them) and we declare deliverance for the afflicted, the captives are released in Jesus' name.

Our lives are not our own. We have been called to live for God and for others. We have been given a commission to embody the character and work of the kingdom to others. No one is left out. No one is excluded. Each is uniquely loved. God wants to reconcile all things to Himself by equipping us to be carriers of His love (2 Cor. 5:18–20).

Jesus commissioned the disciples with this message of the kingdom of God. Jesus ruled (and still rules) with power and authority, and He sent His disciples out to do likewise. He urged them to become friends with the people and to heal the sick (Luke 10:9). He instructed them to proclaim the good news of the kingdom. Upon their return, the disciples reported, 'Even the demons submit to us in your name' (Luke 10:17).

Turn the cup of your life the right way up so it can be filled afresh and overflow. You can become a carrier of the presence of God. You are called and privileged to carry blessings to others.

How do you put that into practice? The next three sessions will be your guide, starting with: how to bless the person in front of you.

P.S.

Have you invited Jesus Christ to be your personal Saviour and the Lord of your life?

If so, now might be a good time to renew your commitment to Jesus.

If not, now is a very good time to extend that invitation. You can speak to Him reverentially, opening your heart to say everything you want to say. Forget any religious jargon—simply start a conversation. He is eagerly waiting for you.

PART II

THE PRACTICE OF BLESSING

Session 4

BLESSING THE PERSON IN FRONT OF YOU

Gather with your group. When everyone is comfortable, work through the material below. Go slowly and reflectively. Honour each other's comments. Watch the video at the recommended point, then continue working through the questions together.

Scripture

> All these are the twelve tribes of Israel, and this is what their father said to them when he blessed them, giving each the blessing appropriate to him. (Gen. 49:28)

Prayer

- **Individual:** Speak the following prayer out loud and reflect on it.
- **Group:** Say this prayer together.

O High King of Heaven,
Have mercy on our Land.
Revive your Church, O Lord.
Your Spirit send for the sake of the poor,
the lost and the broken.
Your Kingdom come; Your will be done
In our nation.
In Jesus' name.
Amen.[2]
(Can also be sung to the tune for 'It Is Well with My Soul.')

Suggested statement from the group leader: 'Let us examine what it means to bless someone whom we may encounter in all kinds of contexts, that they may know the release of the blessing that God desires for them. Roy Godwin has some teaching that will help us reflect on this.'

Play Video: SESSION FOUR

We encourage you to take notes as you watch the video. Feel free to use the space under the Your Notes header following this paragraph. Note anything that you find especially helpful or provokes you to examine the way you view what it means to love God and follow Jesus in the world today.

Your Notes

Review

What helped or provoked you in what Roy shared in the video? Underline the key points in the notes you have made. If you are part of a group, share together, if that would be helpful.

Reflect

What Scripture stories, verses or principles spring to your mind as you reflect on this idea of blessing others in the name of Jesus? Write them in your notes. If you are part of a group, share these with the others, if that would be helpful. Have you had some experience of blessing others that may be encouraging to the rest of the group?

Focus

- **Individual:** The following Key Insights section provides supporting scriptures and a deeper look into the content of this session to supplement what you have already noted.
- **Group:** If you're studying as a group, your group leader will now summarise some of the things you have shared together. Be ready to note any additional points he or she may make that could be helpful to you. The following Key Insights section provides supporting scriptures and some helpful summaries. Use this material to supplement what you have already noted and to aid further discussion. You may find it useful for personal reflection at a later date as well.

Key Insights

As Roy noted, Genesis 12:1–9 is a key passage for our understanding of the biblical idea of blessing.

1. You don't have to be a spiritual giant to speak blessings effectively. Suzanne's story at the end of the session helps illustrate this.

2. There is a structure in our blessing.

- **Name**—We name the person so there is no doubt about who we are addressing.

- **I Bless You**—We have received delegated authority from God to speak blessings that reflect His character.
- **In the Name of Jesus**—We are making it clear to the hearer, the Father and the enemy of our souls that we are ministering blessing under the delegated authority of Jesus.
- **That He**—A mere recitation of a personal blessing is not what we have in mind. God told Aaron to 'put My name on them' and He would then come and bless (see Num. 6:27).
- **May**—Psalm 20:1–5 is an example of declaring the blessing of God. It speaks of protection, plans, desires and victory. It speaks of the whole of their life. Central to it is the word *may*. There is a world of difference between 'He might' and 'that He may.'

3. God desires to give us a redemptive revelation for the life and circumstances of people.

The Message Bible gives a flavour of what that might look like in our lives in 1 Peter 3:8–9.

4. The BLESS acronym helps direct us into well-rounded areas for blessing.

- **B**ody—health, protection, strength; God wants to restore us and renew our health.
- **L**abour—work, reward, security; because God cares for the whole person.
- **E**motional—joy, peace, hope; *health* here means health in the rest of our lives.
- **S**ocial—love, marriage, family, friends; we were created for community.

- **S**piritual—salvation, faith, grace; God desires to renew us in the patterns of our thinking about Him, our purpose in the earth and our future hope. Whoever we are, believer or nonbeliever, He wants us to discover the mind of Christ.

Now let's put the theory into practice as we bless each other.

Your Notes

Bless

As we conclude our session, we will turn to practice and start to learn by doing.

- **Individual:** Read the blessing instructions below—and at some point in the week, seek out a person you feel comfortable sharing with and proclaim the outlined blessing together.
- **Group:** Use the framework outlined below.

Keep in mind that this is just an exercise to help you get started. Blessing is a direct ministry, not a reading out of written words or of liturgy. And remember, some people may feel shy about speaking aloud for a multitude of reasons. Speaking together as a group may be more comfortable for them. The leader of the study should volunteer to be ministered to by the whole group.

The group might speak out these blessings together:

(*Name*), **we bless you in the name of Jesus, that He might** give you life. The abundant life that God desires for you.

PAUSE—COUNT TO TWO

(*Name*), **we bless you in the name of Jesus, that He may** raise a hedge around you. And that you may know His protection over your mind and in all your life circumstances.

PAUSE—COUNT TO TWO

(*Name*), **we bless you in the name of Jesus, that He may** open the eyes of your heart and that you may receive a revelation of the heart, character and purposes of God and the wisdom He has for your life.

PAUSE—COUNT TO TWO

(*Name*), **we bless you in the name of Jesus, that He might** be your comforter and that you may feel the comfort and sustenance of God in your waking and sleeping, working and playing.

PAUSE—COUNT TO TWO

(*Name*), **we bless you in the name of Jesus, that He may** fill you anew, and that you may be a vessel of Holy Spirit–empowered wholeness.

PAUSE—COUNT TO TWO

(*Name*), **we bless you in the name of Jesus, that He may** be continually renewing you, refreshing the patterns of your thinking so that you may be whole and complete, as God intended.

PAUSE—COUNT TO TWO

Amen.

Prayer Idea

- **Individual:** Take a quiet moment to think of an aspect of your life that needs healing or restoration. Then perhaps at some point in the week, seek out a person you feel comfortable with. Share with each other what area you would like to receive blessing for and take it in turns to practise blessing.

- **Group:** The group should be silent for a minute. Take that moment to think of an aspect of *your* life that needs healing or restoration. Then connect with one or two other people. Share very briefly with them what you would like to receive from God. Keep it simple and short—preferably, one sentence, like 'I need healing in my foot' or 'I'm struggling to forgive' or 'I need a job.'

It's better not to share details—and don't start to counsel people who are sharing with you. One person should share, and then the other(s) should bless them. And then the next one and so on. Be careful not to slide into general praying when you are learning to *speak* blessing with authority.

You may like to use this simple framework: 'I bless you, (*Name*), in the name of Jesus that the Father might respond now to (what they just shared).'

Stick with speaking blessing, not praying. Stay focussed, and don't be diverted into praying for broader issues, as can sometimes happen when we gather.

Life Activity

Some of these ideas will perhaps give you the opportunity to bless people face to face. Don't worry if they don't, however. They will still help you cultivate a mindset of blessing and grace.

Seven Days of Blessing

Below are seven simple daily ideas for speaking out blessing that you could use this week. When you do so, you might like to use the following forms of words:

- I bless (*that day's topic*) in the name of Jesus and for His glory.
- I bless (*him, her or them*) in the name of Jesus, that they may know peace, health and a revelation of God through Jesus.

You can expand on these—but they're good starting points.

As your group dismisses and you all go back to your lives, remember to take time to bless the friendships and activities of the place or person that you are blessing—and ask God to bring His kingdom values to the awareness of those there. Sometimes, it will be appropriate to speak out loud—other times, it will just be you and God talking to each other.

MONDAY
Bless your family members—both near and far.

TUESDAY
Bless your workplace or the schools that your children attend.

WEDNESDAY
Bless the streets near where you live—if you can, walk around and quietly bless them that the transforming peace of the Prince of Peace might invade them.

THURSDAY
Bless and pray for someone in your neighbourhood, workplace or activity whom you may see regularly and perhaps even exchange greetings with. Ask God for openings to talk further and to pray for them personally, blessing them appropriately.

FRIDAY

Bless your enemies. It's not easy—but it is biblical. Jesus reminds us to 'love your enemies and pray for those who persecute you' and 'love your enemies, do good to those who hate you' (Matt. 5:44; Luke 6:27).

SATURDAY

Bless a Christian friend. Ask God to reveal to you what you might say in the form of blessing. Don't get religious. Stay relaxed and speak out in faith.

SUNDAY

Bless the Church. As you are perhaps thinking about gathering with your church today, speak blessings over them in Jesus' name, that God might bless His people and increase their witness to His love and grace.

Session 4:
Going
Deeper

BLESSING THE PERSON IN FRONT OF YOU
Further Material for Personal Reading

Daphne, with her big, soft heart, invited Suzanne (not her real name), an obviously troubled woman, to attend the conference we had planned for that weekend, even though we had a long waiting list.

The meetings were full, so Suzanne had to sit near the front, despite her preference for being at the back. The worship one evening was so powerful and the sense of God's presence so overwhelming, that it felt as though heaven and earth had combined to sing God's praise. Suddenly, I noticed Suzanne standing with her head forward. Her face was purple, her eyes looked as though they were going to burst out of her face, and her tongue was distended. Russ Parker, one of the speakers that weekend, had already noticed, and he went straight to her.

He touched her neck and spoke a word and then returned to the speaker's area. I saw her instantly relax. Later, I noticed her with hands in the air and face uplifted, absolutely lost in praise and worship.

At the end of the evening, she came up to me to share her story. When she was eighteen, she decided that she wanted to be a worshipper of God (those were her words). She found a local church and still remained there, decades later. She would sit at the back because she had suffered with depression. Hospitalisation and medication had done little to help, and she stayed visibly depressed. She wanted to be there to honour God, but she didn't want to be off-putting to anyone else.

When she tried to open her mouth to sing, she would immediately have a sensation of being physically choked. She couldn't breathe, and she thought she was going to die. Needless to say, she didn't normally sing. Earlier that evening, she had felt caught up in the worship, but the moment she'd joined in the singing, she'd felt she was being strangled.

Russ spoke very clearly when he went across to her: 'In the name of Jesus, I release you from what is choking you.' Immediately, she could breathe and was free and was able to worship as never before.

The next morning, we held a thanksgiving and testimony meeting to close the conference, and I invited her to share what had happened to her the previous night. That seemed safe, and she looked radiant, but I forgot a principle when in that type of public situation: don't ask people questions when you don't know what the answers are going to be!

'Are things different for you today?' I asked.

'Oh, yes,' she responded. 'My heart is light and I can smile, and I can worship for the first time ever.'

Cheers resounded around the hall. I ventured that she must have slept well. 'No—I couldn't sleep last night for weeping about the pain.'

She began to sob and said that God had revealed to her the root of the choking sensation. It was buried deep in her memory. She remembered it being close to her fourth birthday and she was in the garage of her father's home. She was very frightened. A strange man was very noisily trying to break into the garage.

He finally broke in. He rushed to her side and grabbed her. He lifted and released her from the noose around her neck. The man had saved Suzanne from being hanged from the rafters by her own father. Another few seconds and it would have been too late.

Her identity was scarred by the rejection implicit in her father's attempt to kill and abandon her. She was never to see her father again.

God's intervention the previous evening had reminded her that He had never let go of her. She had immediately been released from the choking sensation and was free to worship and sing her heart out for the first time.

The atmosphere was electric as she shared her story, and there were many tears amongst the congregation. She had much else to heal in her life, but the process had begun.

When I shared that story with a vocal specialist sometime later, she turned away and appeared to wipe tears from her eyes. She composed herself and said that Suzanne's choking issues were consistent with what psychologists knew about responses to trauma. It was wonderful, she said, that Suzanne had been healed.

But then the vocal specialist asked one of those questions that make you want to wince, cry and get angry all at the same time. 'If it is true, as it seems, that the Jesus you speak of has power to heal, how could this lady have been in a church for so long and not be set free before now?'

There are no easy answers to that question, but across the body of Christ we have not always grasped how the Bible reminds us that salvation and healing, blessing and releasing captives are all part of the good news. We have not grasped the full extent of the kingdom message and authority that Jesus proclaimed and now delegates to us. God's heart is still to bless. We are His agents of the kingdom; we are His body.

Jesus had to come to Suzanne's world that day in the same way that He came to a house in Capernaum:

Some men came, bringing to him a paralysed man, carried by four of them. Since they could not get him to Jesus because of the crowd, they made an opening in the roof above Jesus by digging through it and then lowered the mat the man was lying on. When Jesus saw their faith, he said to the paralysed man, 'Son, your sins are forgiven.' …

He said to the man, 'I tell you, get up, take your mat and go home.' He got up, took his mat and walked out in full view of them all. This amazed everyone and they praised God, saying, 'We have never seen anything like this!' (Mark 2:3–5, 10–12)

Salvation and healing are never too far from each other when Jesus enters a house. Jesus said to the sick man, 'I tell you, get up.' The words used here speak of awakening. Jesus said, 'Take your mat.' The mat was symbolic of the illness that had captured the paralytic, but now it no longer held him. He held it, carried it away. He was reigning over it. Out of his brokenness, this man was now strengthened for compassion; out of his pain, he could help others step out of brokenness. The wound became a beauty spot.

Jesus delegated His authority to seventy of His disciples, just as Moses had done to the seventy elders God gave him (Num. 11:16–17). Jesus breathed on His disciples that they might receive the Holy Spirit and sent them out to exercise authority in His name and bring the kingdom of God near to people (Luke 10).

What we believe we're seeing at the heart of what God is doing amongst us is that Jesus left heaven to be 'in the house' here with us on earth. *He brought heaven near to us and empowered us by the Holy Spirit to bring heaven near to others.* Indeed, much of the way that He talks of the work of the kingdom involves pictures of proximity:

- 'The time has come,' he said. 'The kingdom of God has come near. Repent and believe the good news!' (Mark 1:15).
- Heal those there who are ill and tell them, 'The kingdom of God has come near to you' (Luke 10:9).
- Once, on being asked by the Pharisees when the kingdom of God would come, Jesus replied, 'The coming of the kingdom of God is not something that can be observed, nor will people say, "Here it is," or "There it is," because the kingdom of God is in your midst' (Luke 17:20–21).

In Acts 2, we read about the day of Pentecost and the pouring out of the Holy Spirit. Jesus had promised that His disciples would receive power to be His witnesses. They were indeed filled, and fearful Peter spoke to the crowd, and three thousand men turned to the Lord. Two chapters later, in Acts 4:8–12, Peter, filled again, responded to the religious authorities. A few verses later, in a prayer meeting where the disciples prayed for boldness to witness, the place shook and they were filled again.

These experiences reflect the anointings within the Old Testament. To be effective when we bless, as with any other ministry, we need to be refreshed in our anointing of the Holy Spirit.

When we *stand* in God's presence, reminding ourselves of His character and His intent, He releases the Spirit to work afresh and anew in our lives so that we might be *anointed* carriers of His presence. We then *speak* His blessings *out of His presence*.

This was well demonstrated by Moses and Aaron in Leviticus 9:22–24. First, Aaron spoke the blessings of the Lord over the people. But nothing observable happened. Moses took him into the tent of meeting, and then they came out and blessed the people again. *This time, the glory of the Lord appeared to all the people, and fire fell.*

We stand on these promises:

- 'Come near to God and he will come near to you' (James 4:8).
- 'Again Jesus said, "Peace be with you! As the Father has sent me, I am sending you"' (John 20:21).
- 'Heal those there who are ill and tell them, "The kingdom of God has come near to you"' (Luke 10:9).

We are empowered to declare the will of God for people, communities and land. We are His envoys. We deliver the message on His behalf. We take hold of these commissions from God and the promises they contain:

- 'The LORD said to Moses, "Tell Aaron and his sons, 'This is how you are to bless the Israelites. Say to them: "The LORD bless you and keep you; the LORD make his face shine on you and be gracious to you; the LORD turn his face towards you and give you peace." So they will put my name on the Israelites, and I will bless them"' (Num. 6:22–27).
- 'When you enter a house, first say, "Peace to this house"' (Luke 10:5).
- 'Mercy, peace and love be yours in abundance' (Jude 1:2).

In the light of all this, we want to be those whose words nourish many. We may have our church programmes, meetings and crusades, but more than anything we need Jesus to be 'in the house.'

Salvation and healing are never too far from each other when Jesus enters a house.

In the story of the four friends and the sick man, we find clues that 'business as usual' had been superseded. But other clues are embedded in the gospel accounts too. The appearance of the glory of God amidst a throng of singing angels and in the presence of lowly shepherds was a first clue (Luke 2:8–17). The presence of God was identified with the temple, and yet here it was in the countryside. Forgiveness was sought at the temple, and yet here was Jesus offering it to a sick man in a small town, on a mat, in a crowded room littered with bits of roof.

With His impossible-to-measure majesty, God draws near to us. He sends Jesus to come near to the broken and wounded, to sinners and saints. His presence is manifest in compassion, healing, forgiveness, the calming of nature and His return from death. When the presence of God is amongst us, we too should expect extraordinary miracles.

When we bless someone in Jesus' name, even when we really don't know what we are doing, we open that person and their circumstances to the present, powerful workings of God.

We read that God spoke to Moses and explained blessing like this: 'So *they* will put my name on the Israelites, and *I* will bless them' (Num. 6:27). Father and children working together.

Foundations of Blessing

We have learned that God still longs to bless people.

- We are blessed by God.
- Then we bless others because we know God wants to bless them.
- Blessing is wrapped up in the good news of the kingdom of God.

Here is a simple and clear framework for blessing a person in front of you:

(Name), I bless you in the name of Jesus, that God may …

Let's look at that more closely.

1. Name

It is important to identify the person by name. Use their first name, if possible.

2. I bless you

Blessing someone is not the same as asking God to bless them. That's *intercession*, and it is important that we do that. Blessing someone, though, means you are standing in your role as a priest of God, looking them straight in the eye and effectively saying, 'God wants to bless you out of His goodness, and I agree with His desire for you.' That is heaven coming to earth! Through you, heaven and earth are aligned with the Father's will to do good to that person.

As you come to pronounce the desire of God to bless, the power is not found in empty words but in the response of God to your proclamation as one who has been given delegated authority. It's not that your words are magic, but that they carry authority as envoys for God. The blessed person's needs will not be met by you; it is God's blessing alone that can satisfy them.

'God wants to bless you out of His goodness, and I agree with His desire for you.' That is heaven coming to earth!

3. In the name of Jesus

When we bless others in Jesus' name, we are trusting Him to come and 'hallow' His name by releasing the fullness of who He is into their lives, causing Him to be called holy.

When we bless others, we are leaning on Jesus' mercy and compassion. Part of the promise of His character relates to His authority—He is the King of all kings. As part of our commitment to Him, we honour and affirm Him as Lord, and we recognise no other ultimate authority. In speaking in His name, we are coming with His authority to address all that is broken or in need of renewal in the lives of people, communities and physical ground.

While on a ministry trip to the Eastern Mediterranean, I was being nudged by God that He was going to teach me more about spiritual authority when I returned home. When I came back, I was surprised to see a rather fine—although unusual—chair. It was a gift from a retired craftsman whom Daphne had met during a prayer trip.

She had commented on the unusual seat she'd spied in his family home. He had explained that he had been producing perfect replicas of what was in Roman Empire times called 'the seat of authority.' It was collapsible so that a magistrate's servant might take it to the centre of town, and it was marked with a Roman emblem. When the magistrate sat in the seat of authority, his words carried the full force of the emperor himself. As soon as he left the seat, he was no more than a man amongst men.

I learned so much through this gift. I am seated with Christ in the heavenly places, and so are you as a believer. His name is our 'seat,' in terms of authority. Found in Him, we can speak normal words that are clothed in all of heaven's delegated authority. That's where we need to be when we bless others. Practically speaking, it helps to prepare ourselves each day, or before each encounter, by reminding ourselves of our correct seated position!

4. That God

All blessing depends on the faithfulness and kindness of God. It does not depend on our performance but on His. That's why it's always important to cry out to Him from the depths of our being something like this: 'Help, Lord. I'm going to bless this person in the name of Jesus. Will You please come to them and keep Your promise that when I bless in Your name, You will bless them?'

Our words in themselves are unlikely to carry the power to change people's lives. The name of Jesus, on the other hand, carries all authority. So, when I bless, it is in order that He might break in and confirm the words with signs following. That's how the Lord explained the ceremonial blessing to Aaron: *Say the words that put My name on the people, and I will come behind you and bless the people.*

If we were to communicate to a deaf person that we blessed them, they might thank us. On the other hand, if we were able to communicate to them, 'We bless you in the name of *Jesus*,' we would have invoked the promise of the Lord to come and do wonderful things in that person's life. If we were to say, 'I bless your hearing,' I can't imagine it having much effect. But we have repeatedly seen the effect of blessing deaf ears in Jesus' name. They have been opened for so many!

5. May

That God may … what? There will always be an element of simply waiting on God and listening for a prompt from the Holy Spirit as to what would be appropriate to speak; or we may sense or see in our mind's eye the blessing that He has for a particular person or people. God may give us discernment, a word of wisdom or a word of knowledge. Any of these may aid us as we speak, and we might bless like this:

> I bless you in the name of Jesus that your eyes may be so fixed on Him that other things that want to take your eyes in other directions may fall away. That you may gaze upon His beauty, that you may have eyes for nothing but Him. That you may be transfixed by the One who looks at you and says—you keep looking at Me, and I'll keep looking at you.

Be aware that sometimes there is an immediate response, but for others there might be an unfolding over minutes, hours, days or weeks. God gently and mercifully goes behind their defences and starts a work. Some will need to repent. In blessing them, we are not blessing their *deeds*—we're blessing them for change.

The question of 'What shall we bless them with?' is the same one we all ask every time. The safety net is that when we bless in Jesus' name, and if we stick to the Scripture's message, we are not going to get it wrong.

One of the helpful ways to look for content when blessing is to search the Scriptures for the word *may*. Psalm 20 offers a good example of Scripture that we can use to speak blessing over people, as it contains the word *may*, not in a tentative sense, but in a strongly positive, 'this is what God desires to do' way.

> May the LORD answer you when you are in distress;
>   may the name of the God of Jacob protect you.
> May he send you help from the sanctuary
>   and grant you support from Zion.
> May he remember all your sacrifices
>   and accept your burnt offerings.
> May he give you the desire of your heart
>   and make all your plans succeed.
> May we shout for joy over your victory
>   and lift up our banners in the name of our God.
> May the LORD grant all your requests. (Ps. 20:1–5)

It's a great section of Scripture to turn into a blessing. For example, you might say, 'I bless you in the name of Jesus, that God may answer you in the day of trouble and that He may do it so clearly that you may know without any question that it's Him.'

You see how to do it? Another example might be, 'I bless you in the name of Jesus that the name of the God of Jacob may protect you. That you may be safe—that you may be secure. I bless you that He may send you help when needed. I bless you in the name of Jesus that He may grant your heart's desire and fulfil all your plans.'

We need to ensure that we do not overly spiritualise the person in front of us. They are a whole human being, and God longs to bless that whole person. 'May your whole spirit, soul and body be kept blameless' (1 Thess. 5:23).

Remember the BLESS acronym from earlier in this session? It can help us as we consider how to bless someone:

- **B**ody—health, protection, strength; God wants to restore us and renew our health.
- **L**abour—work, reward, security; because God cares for the whole person.
- **E**motional—joy, peace, hope; health here means health in the rest of our lives.
- **S**ocial—love, marriage, family, friends; we were created for community.
- **S**piritual—salvation, faith, grace; God desires to renew us in the patterns of our thinking about Him, our purpose in the earth and our future hope. Whoever we are, believer or nonbeliever—He wants us to discover the mind of Christ.

A caution: we must always act with sensitivity to the person and without even a shadow of manipulation. The prophet Isaiah reminds us that God gave him (and may desire to give us) 'a well-instructed tongue, to know the word that sustains the weary' (Isa. 50:4).

It is a wonderful privilege to bless another person. We should be eager to bless.

To whom might you show mercy? How might you cultivate good? Acts of blessing work alongside words of blessing. The mercy of God lifts a weight off us completely. We are encouraged to cast our cares upon Him. By extension, our small acts of compassion for others—gardening, transportation, a listening ear, simply having patience in the face of difficult behaviour—are acts of both mercy and blessing. We do them with no agenda, not asking for anything back. But they are an instrument of the Holy Spirit, a means of grace, and more often than not, they provoke people to ask about Jesus.

The shalom prayer of peace that Jesus commissioned His disciples to pray (Luke 10:5) is helpful to us. The word *shalom* is rich in meaning. As you think about speaking blessing over someone, you might want to consider what the following words linked to shalom might mean in the life of that person. It may soon become clear what you should pronounce in the light of that person's circumstance:

- Peace
- Harmony
- Wholeness
- Completeness
- Prosperity
- Welfare
- Tranquillity

So if you wanted to bless with respect to harmony: 'I bless you in the name of Jesus that He may grant you a strengthening of relationships, restoration of broken friendships and fruitfulness together as friends.'

There is a common-sense wisdom that also prevails when we speak blessing. Imagine you are blessing someone with a respiratory infection: 'I bless you in the name of Jesus that He may heal your respiratory system. I bless your immune system in Jesus' name, that it might rise up and that your sinuses may become clear.'

The Simplicity of Blessing

You may be tempted to think that the miracles you have read about happen to 'other people' and that those who bless are from a spiritual elite. Many of those whom the Lord uses are, however, simply obedient disciples. Sometimes God teases us!

My new secretary had been with us for a brief time when she walked by some visitors. One woman hailed her and asked whether it was true that God healed people today.

Yes, it was true, she said.

How would you heal someone with broken bones, the visitor asked?

My secretary responded with 'I've no personal experience of that, but I know what Roy does. He says something like, "Broken bones, I bless you in Jesus' name and command you to be perfectly healed."'

Thank you, said the guest.

An hour later, the visitor asked to see her again. She explained that she was having a retreat before a hospital visit to have a badly broken and immobile thumb operated on. However, she had suddenly realised that her thumb was now mobile and pain-free since hearing those words. Moreover, one of her big toes had been broken for years, and that too was now healed.

Most of us will step into the arena of blessing and proclamation with some trepidation. What should we say? Will it work? Am I headed for a huge embarrassment? My prayer is that you have understood a way and a structure for blessing the person in front of you. Here is good news—when we don't seem to get it right, God steps in and blesses anyway.

What about blessing people who are not standing in front of you? Your neighbours, street, town? We will journey through this in the next session.

Session 5

BLESSING COMMUNITIES, REGIONS AND NATIONS

Gather with your group. When everyone is comfortable, work through the material below. Go slowly and reflectively. Honour each other's comments. Watch the video at the recommended point, then continue working through the questions together.

Scripture

> And if you faithfully obey the voice of the LORD your God, being careful to do all his commandments that I command you today, the LORD your God will set you high above all the nations of the

earth. And all these blessings shall come upon you and overtake you, if you obey the voice of the LORD your God. Blessed shall you be in the city, and blessed shall you be in the field. Blessed shall be the fruit of your womb and the fruit of your ground and the fruit of your cattle, the increase of your herds and the young of your flock. Blessed shall be your basket and your kneading bowl. Blessed shall you be when you come in, and blessed shall you be when you go out.

The LORD will cause your enemies who rise against you to be defeated before you. They shall come out against you one way and flee before you seven ways. The LORD will command the blessing on you in your barns and in all that you undertake. And he will bless you in the land that the LORD your God is giving you. (Deut. 28:1–8 ESV)

Prayer

Pray the following prayer, which is based on Psalm 103.

- **Individual:** Speak out the psalm.
- **Group:** The leader will read the lines in lighter text, inviting the whole group to declare together the bold lines.

Praise the Lord, O people of God,
May we never forget all Your benefits.
Forgive us our sins
and heal all our diseases.

PAUSE FOR TWO SECONDS

He has redeemed our lives from the pit.
Crown us with love and compassion, O God.
He satisfies our desires with good things;
Father of Creation, renew our passion.
The Lord works righteousness;
make us the champions of the oppressed.

PAUSE FOR TWO SECONDS

He made known His ways to Moses.
Make Your deeds known today.
The Lord is compassionate and gracious.
Help us to be slow to anger, abounding in love.
He does not treat us as our sins deserve.
May we be carriers of mercy.

PAUSE FOR TWO SECONDS

For as high as the heavens are above the earth,
so great is His love for those who fear Him;
As far as the east is from the west,
so far has He removed our transgressions from us.
As a father has compassion on his children,
so the Lord has compassion on those who fear Him.
Amen and amen.

Suggested statement from the group leader: 'In today's video, we will examine how we might pray for communities, regions and nations. This will be rooted in our understanding of God's desire for creation and His compassion for us.'

Play Video: SESSION FIVE

We encourage you to take notes as you watch the video. Feel free to use the space under the Your Notes header following this paragraph. Note anything that you find especially helpful or provokes you to examine the way you view what it means to love God and follow Jesus in the world today.

Your Notes

Review

What helped or provoked you in what Roy shared in the video? Underline the key points in the notes you made. If you are part of a group, share together, if that would be helpful.

Reflect

Do you have any additional insights about the nature of God's blessing for our localities? What Scripture stories, verses or principles spring to your mind as you reflect on this topic? Write them in your notes. If you are part of a group, share together, if that would be helpful.

Focus

- **Individual:** The following Key Insights section provides supporting scriptures and a deeper look into the content of this session to supplement what you have already noted.
- **Group:** If you're studying as a group, your group leader will now summarise some of the things that you have shared together. Be ready to note any additional points he or she may make that could be helpful to you. The following Key Insights section provides supporting scriptures and a deeper look into the content of this session. Use this material to supplement what you have already noted and to aid further discussion. You may find it useful for personal reflection at a later date as well.

Key Insights

1. There is a geography of blessing.

God is passionate about us as individuals, but He is also looking on the totality of His creation. Deuteronomy 11:11–12 tells us that 'the eyes of the LORD your God are continually on it from the beginning of the year to its end.' King David majestically reminds us that 'the earth is the LORD's and everything in it' (Ps. 24:1).

2. God works naturally and supernaturally to reveal to us that which may be troubling our areas, regions or nations.

God will also prompt us about what we might pray positively for the places where we live and what blessings we might declare.

3. In this session, we will highlight the aspects of communal life over which we might declare the blessings of God.

This is more than interceding for a place—it is the declaration of God's blessing for that place or people. Remember that we are declaring the Word of the Lord for people and places and His delight in showing His love, grace and mercy.

4. It may be instructive at this point to remind ourselves about the kind of places where Jesus was found introducing the presence of the kingdom and bringing the tangible blessing of God through the declaration of the kingdom of God:

- At a wedding in Cana
- With the fishermen at their work

- In the house of a civil servant
- In the everyday lives of His close followers
- Debating in the marketplace
- Teaching on the mountain
- In the temple
- In the company of the unloved, the lost, the poor and the rejected outcasts
- In the synagogues
- In places of idolatrous worship, such as near Samaritan holy places or pagan healing pools
- By Himself, talking to the Father

Jesus was everywhere, His intimacy with God provoking involvement with people. Like the Levitical priests of old:

- He stood in the presence of God.
- He carried the presence of God.
- He pronounced the blessings of God.

Your Notes

Your Notes (continued)

Prayer

As we conclude our session, we turn to prayer, talking to the God who blesses and declaring our own blessing and thankfulness towards Him.

Prayer Idea

Look at the everyday places listed in the following Life Activity section, and see if you can identify one of those places close to where you are meeting your group.

- **Individual:** Do you have a connection with one or more of the places mentioned in the Life Activity section? Choose a place and speak blessings into different aspects of the life of the place. You could mention named places, specific people or people with responsibilities, such as schoolteachers, policemen or police-women, judges or those working in social services. Think about how you might proclaim blessings over this place during the rest of the week.

- **Group:** Your leader will now guide you through a prayer activity. This will be 'learning by doing' as you think about how you might proclaim blessings during the rest of the week.

Life Activity

Blessing and Prayer—Walking Guide

See if you can walk by or visit any of the following areas during the next few weeks. Speak as you feel led, but use the blessings below as an anchor for prayers as well.

AT A SCHOOL

We bless this school in the name of Jesus, that it may be a secure and safe place for teachers and pupils. We bless the children's capacity to learn and play and develop relationships. We bless them that they might have an opportunity to hear about Jesus and His love for them. We bless them to grow like mighty oak trees for the nations to marvel and see.

AT A FACTORY, WORKSHOP OR OFFICES

In the name of Jesus, we bless those who work here, that they may know joy in their work and friendship in their workplace, and that they may work well and effectively. We bless all the industry in this area, that it may continue to be a good means of income for many. We bless this place, that safety and care may increase for all those who work here.

AT A TOWN SQUARE OR MARKET

We bless this place in the name of Jesus and all who gather here. We bless those who work here, that God may prosper their businesses. We bless the conversations which take place, that they may be enriched by the wisdom of the Holy Spirit. We bless these streets, that they may be places of community and welcome.

BY A PHARMACY

We bless the health of the people in this locality, that they may be strong and well. In Jesus' name we resist any sickness or disease which seeks to invade this town, and to every person here we say: in Jesus' name be strong, be healthy. To any who are sick right now, we bless you in Jesus' name that you may have a speedy recovery.

AT A CHURCH

We bless all the Christians in this place in the name of Jesus, for those who are part of the congregation here or who meet with other Christians elsewhere, that each one may be like a light shining out for all people to see. We bless the Holy Spirit–given gifts of the Christians in this place, that He may flow like a river through each one of us.

AT A POLICE STATION OR COURT

We bless those who keep watch over the safety and integrity of this place in the name of Jesus. We also bless those who seek to ensure that there is justice for all. In Jesus' name we bless those who seek to restore those who fall and fail. We bless the local churches to be part of this process. We bless all of these people, that they may know integrity and act without favouritism.

AT A TOWN HALL OR CIVIC OFFICES

We bless in the name of Jesus all who work here and around this community to ensure that life is well ordered for all who live here. May the Holy Spirit be at work to promote beauty and joy as part of the heritage of this place.

AT A CULTURAL CENTRE—VENUE, GALLERY, THEATRE OR GARDENS

We bless this place in the name of the God of beauty and creativity that we find expressed in Jesus, that it may be somewhere from which culture will spring to bring glory to His name. We bless those who create things of beauty and craftsmanship that bring joy, delight and wonder. May the art and creativity of this place speak of His character and compassion.

As your group dismisses and you all go back to your lives, always remember that you are *speaking* blessing, not *praying* blessing. You are walking in authority to bless because you carry the name and the Spirit of Jesus with you.

Practice makes perfect!

Session 5:
Going
Deeper

BLESSING COMMUNITIES, REGIONS AND NATIONS

Further Material for Personal Reading

Many of us instinctively understand how to pray for or with other people, but what is the biblical pattern when it comes to praying for, or blessing, named geographical areas? And what do we think that achieves?

Fundamentally, we are obeying Jesus by praying for the kingdom to come on a specific part of planet Earth and that God's will might be done there as it is in heaven. We are praying that the presence of God will be more apparent and that it will touch every area of life and existence in that area. We are praying that revelation of Jesus as Saviour and Lord will fall upon the people there. We are praying that God will prepare hearts to receive His Word, understand it and respond to it. We are also praying that He will touch every aspect of creation that is found in that place.

This 'local and regional' prayer and blessing is found in multiple contexts in Scripture.

IN A HOSTILE PAGAN CITY

Also, seek the peace and prosperity *of the city* to which I have carried you into exile. Pray to the LORD for it, because if it prospers, you too will prosper. (Jer. 29:7)

FOR THE ISRAELITE PEOPLE

At the time of sacrifice, the prophet Elijah stepped forward and prayed: 'LORD, the God of Abraham, Isaac and Israel, *let it be known today that you are God in Israel* and that I am your servant and have done all these things at your command.' (1 Kings 18:36)

FOR THE CITY OF PEACE

Pray for the peace of *Jerusalem*:
'May those who love you be secure.' (Ps. 122:6)

FOR THOSE STRUCTURES AND PEOPLE WHO CAN BE GOOD SHEPHERDS FOR THEIR PEOPLE

I urge, then, first of all, that petitions, prayers, *intercession and thanksgiving be made for all people*—for kings and all those in authority, that we may live peaceful and quiet lives in all godliness and holiness. This is good, and pleases God our Saviour, who wants all people to be saved. (1 Tim. 2:1–4)

FOR THE HOUSEHOLDS AND TOWNS OF JUDAH AND GALILEE

When you enter a house, first say, *'Peace to this house.'* (Luke 10:5)

GOD'S PLAN FOR THE NATIONS TODAY

This, then, is how you should pray:

'Our Father in heaven,

hallowed be your name,

your kingdom come,

your will be done,

    on earth as it is in heaven.' (Matt. 6:9–10)

For God was pleased to have all his fullness dwell in him, and through him to reconcile to himself all things, whether things on earth or things in heaven, by making peace through his blood, shed on the cross.

    Once you were alienated from God and were enemies in your minds because of your evil behaviour. (Col. 1:19–21)

The passages above alert us to the fact that these prayers were often being offered for places and people who might not have acknowledged the claims of God and Jesus yet. These prayers were part of the impulse of God to reconcile all things to Himself.

GOD'S PLAN FOR THE NATIONS IN THE FUTURE

For the earth will be filled with the knowledge of the glory of the LORD. (Hab. 2:14)

The kingdom of the world has become

    the kingdom of our Lord and of his Messiah,

    and he will reign for ever and ever. (Rev. 11:15)

God knows and cares about every street, village, town, city, region and nation. Bethel is one of the locations spoken of in the Old Testament as a special place where God did certain things. Likewise, Bethlehem is mentioned as the place where the Messiah would be born. The Valley of Megiddo, the Mount of Olives, Mount Zion and more are places specified by God as spots where He would do great works.

Let us not forget Jerusalem, where world-shaking events have happened and will take place and where the presence of God will be known and celebrated. When you go up to Jerusalem, you are to sing the Song of Ascents, because when you get there, you find that it isn't the same as other places. God has chosen to do something in that place. The Bible also tells us that one day there will be a renewal of the earth and the New Jerusalem will come down. There will be a new city that will have no need of the sun or moon because the Lamb will be in the midst (Rev. 21:23).

Of course, God is everywhere, and you cannot escape His presence. But the Scriptures also suggest that He sometimes chooses to manifest Himself in particular ways and at particular times in specific places.

I believe that when Moses saw the burning bush (Ex. 3), it was the only bush that was burning. It was *that* bush—it was a specific bush. This didn't in any way diminish the fact that God was everywhere. God told him, 'Take your shoes off, Moses, for this is holy ground.' We're aware that there is a recognition of the manifestation of the holiness of God, and we too had better be careful to recognise it and careful as we approach it.

God's desire is to transform lives, communities and nations as His merciful, loving, righteous presence is welcomed. He stirs up His people to serve His purposes in intercession and blessing. Many of us haven't even formed a basic strategy for praying for our own communities, let alone for a foreign nation. And yet God said, 'Ask of me, and I will make the nations your heritage' (Ps. 2:8 ESV).

As we look to God's loving heart and His Word, we find a longing rising within us that every part of the earth may become holy ground.

How to Bless Communities, Regions and Nations

We have seen how the BLESS acronym can help us define areas of life appropriate for speaking blessings. Another way of understanding the blessing of God is found in the word *shalom*. This Hebrew word includes ideas of peace, wholeness, tranquillity, welfare and prosperity (in the classic sense). When we connect prayer uttered to God with the speaking out of blessing to mankind, we invite the inbreak of heaven on earth.

Aligning our lives so that we rightly express God's loving heart means heaven touches earth. This is the agreement that God is seeking in His mission to send His kingdom here. We experience this in times of revival.

Again, the blessing over communities found in Psalm 129:8 is very helpful: 'The blessing of the LORD be upon you! We bless you in the name of the LORD!' (ESV). Let's break that down into composite steps.

'The blessing of the LORD be upon you' might be seen as nothing more than nice words, but what if they are used as an invocation? A heartfelt petition, calling upon the Lord to come and bless the inhabitants? *The partnership and constant interweaving of prayer, invocation and blessing?* They should be inseparable activities.

As we look to God's loving heart and His Word, we find a longing rising within us that every part of the earth may become holy ground.

'The blessing of the LORD be upon you' is a prayer and an invocation for the goodness of the Lord to come upon a community, region, nation or physical ground, and it is what allows us to speak out the blessing. And notice the dynamism of the blessing—that it should be *upon* them.

When we then add *we* to it, saying, 'We bless you in the name of the LORD,' we are releasing the power of agreement into the community. We are boldly affirming that we, being only flesh, *are in alignment and full agreement* with God's desire to bless them. We join in with God's blessing by adding our own. Blessing is pronounced over them both from heaven and from earth. The life of the kingdom of God is being expressed. This is God's children walking as they should, part of the royal priesthood.

A Simple Pattern of Prayer and Blessing over Areas, Regions and Nations

Praying for places involves:

- Aligning our heart with God's purpose that His kingdom should come to a specific community/place, region or nation.
- Urgently inviting the breaking in of His kingdom today with power to tear down strongholds and release captives.
- Asking that wisdom and integrity would come upon the political and business leaders.
- Asking that the benefits of God's rule would be released throughout the communities and homes.
- Asking that an invasion of God's peace, righteousness and justice would come into every aspect of the place.

- Asking for an increase in care for the poor and downtrodden of society.
- Asking for revelation of Jesus into unbelieving hearts and homes.

We can follow these by speaking out blessing over the area by saying, 'The blessing of the Lord be upon you! And we bless you in the name of Jesus.'

We can then use the BLESS acronym and prayers for shalom to bless every area of life in the region we are interceding for.

When we connect prayer uttered to God with the speaking out of blessing to mankind, we invite the inbreak of heaven on earth.

We will want to use the same practice over our immediate family, neighbours, work colleagues, students and so on. You may find it better to do this in private if you're going to do it often. It probably wouldn't be appropriate to knock on their door every day to bless them! Although I know people who do just that.

Note: our attention must be fixed on the character of God. We concentrate on His purpose, the teaching of Jesus about praying in the kingdom and His desire to bless. We focus on His will to tear down strongholds of wickedness and release captives of darkness, addiction, hopelessness and lostness. We agree with God's willingness to win unbelieving men and women by a mighty revelation of His love expressed so purely and fully in the person of Jesus. Surely our heart wants to burst with joy!

As we turn to look at Him, we reject every focus on wickedness. Jesus, the light of the world, is the total antidote to darkness. Even the shadows flee when He draws near.

Transformation takes place in communities, regions and nations when God overshadows them and releases His presence and blessing. In the same way, transformation takes place in every heart that turns towards Him in surrender and worship.

Walking in Intentional Blessing

There is something so powerful about walking across the land, praying over it and speaking blessing into it. And the Bible provides plenty of support for this.

God told Abram (Abraham) to arise and walk through the length and breadth of the Promised Land (Gen. 13:17). The psalmist recorded the normal blessing which could be placed upon a community or city: 'The blessing of the LORD be upon you; we bless you in the name of the LORD' (Ps. 129:8 NKJV). Solomon wrote, 'Through the blessing of the upright a city is exalted' (Prov. 11:11). And Isaiah proclaimed, 'How beautiful on the mountains are the feet of him who brings good tidings, making peace heard; who brings good news, making salvation heard; who says to Zion, your God reigns!' (Isa. 52:7 MKJV).

Jesus modelled life and ministry for us, and we see numerous encounters with individuals as He walked. The sinful, the sick and the lost. Mothers with their babies begging for blessing.

In the early Church, we see the apostles and disciples continuing the practice of Jesus, walking and stopping to minister to those they met, such as when Peter and John stopped for the lame beggar as they walked to the prayer meeting, or when Philip met the Ethiopian in the chariot. At one time, the people in the city used to put the sick out in the streets so that at least Peter's shadow might overshadow some of them (Acts 5:15).

We might have practised prayer walking, but few have been doing blessing walking. The purpose is that we stand in agreement with God's desire that His kingdom should come to that place, that people should have the opportunity to taste and see that the Lord is good, and that people would be open to the revelation of who Jesus is.

Beautiful Feet

My friend Mike Hey has been developing various ministries of blessing in Australia and beyond. His experiences are encouraging and so exciting.

Mike had been speaking with a local leader about walking the city with Jesus and speaking blessings. The leader was quite unsure about it being biblical. 'Doesn't blessing properly belong inside the church building?' he asked. Mike encouraged him to find another man to walk with him so they could experience it for themselves. He found a friend who would go with him.

They hadn't gone far when a woman's voice sounded across the busy street: 'Hey, you two, wait a moment.' They waited, wondering what was going on. When she caught up with them, she asked whether they were both Christians. Surprised, they said they were, at which point the woman said that God had instructed her to say to them, 'Don't be afraid; He has called *both* of you to bless the city, and there will be a release of great blessing.' What particularly impacted them was that God had chosen an aboriginal woman, historically and culturally identified with the physical ground, to speak with them in this way. Since then, they have continued to walk and speak blessings.

Mike has taken many people through the material found in this book. He lives close to an area of a city that is being developed with new housing estates and parks. Walking with another believer and blessing the homes and people they meet has produced much fruit. Some people have turned to the Lord, some are seeking and many are blessed. He has discovered how easy it is to offer to bless people and places such as homes and families. Some of those he has met when walking have now become hosts for family, friends and neighbours who would like to know more.

Caring for people has very practical implications too. Sometimes they find themselves using their gifts to help, including finding and fitting a kitchen at no cost for someone who wanted to invite neighbours around to learn more and be blessed.

Mike has created a helpful framework for walking to intentionally bless a neighbourhood. He calls them his TIPS:

> **T**rust God
> **I**ntentionally bless
> **P**ray as you go
> **S**how and share Jesus

Your Own Blessings Walks

If you would like to practise this yourself, here are some guidelines from Mike for how to prepare and conduct your walks. Your goal as you go is to be Christ's presence. Love and listen. Enjoy relationships. See God at work. Show and share Jesus. Serve people in His name. Speak Jesus.

Here are five headings to consider as you prepare to go on your first blessings walk.

Personal

- Abide in Christ, trusting Him and leaning into Him, and prayerfully align yourself with His purpose to bless people.
- Find a friend to walk with and acknowledge that there is authority when two or more agree together in Jesus' name.
- Prayerfully decide together where you will walk. Share a scripture together and look for indications that might help you with that decision.

Preparation

- Search for a good venue in that neighbourhood to invite people for a next step. A coffee shop, a place for a BBQ, a home that is open to you etc.
- Plan times together when you might go there.

Practise

- Walk together and learn from each other as you walk.
- Breathe out blessings over homes, people and families as you walk.
- Interact with anyone you encounter.
- Tell them why you are there and what you are doing.
- Keep it simple and make a regular time to walk.
- Always build on relationships.

- Plan a time and a place for those who are interested to learn more about Jesus.

Demonstrate

- Model a lifestyle of blessing: be present, listen, enjoy relationships, see God at work, show and share Jesus.
- Demonstrate a culture of hospitality: invite people to a BBQ, a coffee at a cafe, a meal in your home.
- Go on a discipleship journey: hear and obey Jesus; help others to hear and obey Jesus.
- Encourage others to do the things listed above too.

Remember

- You belong to Jesus, and He is building His Church with you!
- Bless everyone in Jesus' name to see transformation.
- Be on a quest to make disciples who will make disciples, so God may multiply vibrant communities of Jesus followers.

God desires us to pray for communities, regions and nations. As God's children, we have a calling and the authority to speak God's blessings over them.

Creation, too, is caught up in the redemptive work of our heavenly Father through Jesus Christ. We will learn about that and its implications for blessing the ground in the next session.

Session 6

BLESSING PHYSICAL GROUND

Gather with your group. When everyone is comfortable, work through the material below. Go slowly and reflectively. Honour each other's comments. Watch the video at the recommended point, then continue working through the questions together.

Scripture

> *You* visit the earth and water it;
>> *you* greatly enrich it;
> the river of God is full of water;
>> *you* provide their grain,
>> for so *you* have prepared it.

You water its furrows abundantly,
     settling its ridges,
softening it with showers,
     and blessing its growth.
You crown the year with your bounty;
     your wagon tracks overflow with abundance.
The pastures of the wilderness overflow,
     the hills gird themselves with joy,
the meadows clothe themselves with flocks,
     the valleys deck themselves with grain,
          they shout and sing together for joy. (Ps. 65:9–13 ESV)

Prayer

- **Individual:** Speak out and reflect on the following prayer.
- **Group:** Say the following prayer together.

For the majestic valley
We rejoice and
We thank You
For the polluted river
We seek Your forgiveness
And prophetic voice
That it may flourish again
For the flower that blooms
Bringing joy
We thank You
For the barren field

or the inhumane factory farm we repent
May we treat all these things as You intended
The earth is Yours and we will bless You for it
The earth is Yours and we will bless it in Your name
The earth is Yours and we will rejoice in it
Lord—heal the land.

Suggested statement from the group leader: 'Today we will look at our call to bless the creation that we have been placed in, and the land in particular. When the Scripture tells us that God is reconciling all things to Himself (Col. 1:19–20), what might that mean for us regarding how we act, pray and bless? Roy Godwin has some teaching that will help us reflect on this.'

Play Video: SESSION SIX

We encourage you to take notes as you watch the video. Feel free to use the space under the two following Your Notes headers. Note anything that you find especially helpful or provokes you to examine the way you view what it means to love God and follow Jesus in the world today.

Your Notes

Your Notes (continued)

Review

What helped or provoked you in what Roy shared in the video? Underline the key points in the notes you made. If you are part of a group, share together, if that would be helpful.

Reflect

Do you have any additional insights about the character of God and why He would desire to bless us? What Scripture stories, verses or principles spring to your mind as you reflect on these topics? Write them in your notes. If you are part of a group, share together, if that would be helpful.

Focus

- **Individual:** The following Key Insights section provides supporting scriptures and a deeper look into the content of this session to supplement what you have already noted.

- **Group:** If you're studying as a group, your group leader will now summarise some of the things that you have shared together. Be ready to note any additional points he or she may make that could be helpful to you. The following Key Insights section provides supporting scriptures and a deeper look into the content of this session. Use this material to supplement what you have already noted and to aid further discussion. You may find it useful for personal reflection at a later date as well.

Key Insights

1. It was good.

It is worth noting that God has placed us in a creation that He calls good (Gen. 1). We are praying for its restoration to its created purpose. It has value in the eyes of God. We can feel tempted to be 'against' everything when we pray, but God is calling us to be *for* the re-creating of the world according to His purpose, desire and wisdom.

As we pray and listen to His voice, God may reveal to us root causes of negative spiritual issues in our locality. We may also discover insights through natural means, such as historical research or observation. We can combine these two in what we might call informed blessing or informed intercession. This helps us 'test the spirits' and not be held captive to the unexamined insights of an individual.

2. What may be polluting the land and the locality?

CURSES

> The land is full of adulterers;
>> because of the curse the land lies parched
>> and the pastures in the wilderness are withered. (Jer. 23:10)

BLOODSHED AND VIOLENCE

> Do not pollute the land where you are. Bloodshed pollutes the land, and atonement cannot be made for the land on which blood has been shed, except by the blood of the one who shed it. Do not defile the land where you live and where I dwell, for I, the LORD, dwell among the Israelites. (Num. 35:33–34)

BROKEN COVENANTS

> The earth is defiled by its people;
>> they have disobeyed the laws,
> violated the statutes
>> and broken the everlasting covenant. (Isa. 24:5)

SIN

> How long will the land lie parched
>> and the grass in every field be withered?
> Because those who live in it are wicked,
>> the animals and birds have perished.
> Moreover, the people are saying,
>> 'He will not see what happens to us.' (Jer. 12:4)

UNFAITHFULNESS AND IDOLATRY

They sacrificed their sons
and their daughters to false gods.
They shed innocent blood,
the blood of their sons and daughters,
whom they sacrificed to the idols of Canaan,
and the land was desecrated by their blood. (Ps. 106:37–38)

3. God suggests that He will bless the locality of those who honour Him.

He will love you and bless you and increase your numbers. He will bless the fruit of your womb, the crops of your land—your grain, new wine and oil—the calves of your herds and the lambs of your flocks in the land that he swore to your ancestors to give you. (Deut. 7:13)

Ask these questions of yourselves:

- Where can we bless?
- What sin can we renounce in ourselves?
- How can we bring peace?
- What does it mean to embody holiness?
- What do we covenant to do because of Jesus?

Your Notes

Prayer

As we conclude our session, we turn to prayer, talking to the God who blesses and declaring our gratitude and thankfulness towards Him. You can use the following prayer and/or the prayer idea below it.

- **Individual:** Speak out the following psalm, pausing before each bolded section.
- **Group:** Read the bolded lines in the following psalm together.

Praise the Lord, my soul.
Lord my God, You are very great;
You are clothed with splendour and majesty.

The Lord wraps Himself in light as with a garment;
He stretches out the heavens like a tent
and lays the beams of His upper chambers on their waters.
He makes the clouds His chariot
and rides on the wings of the wind.

He makes grass grow for the cattle, and plants for people to
  cultivate—bringing forth food from the earth: wine that
  gladdens human hearts, oil to make their faces shine and
  bread that sustains their hearts.

How many are Your works, Lord! In wisdom You made them
  all; the earth is full of Your creatures.

All creatures look to You
to give them their food at the proper time.
When You give it to them
they gather it up;
when You open Your hand,
they are satisfied with good things.

When You send Your Spirit,
they are created,
and You renew the face of the earth.
May the glory of the Lord endure forever;
may the Lord rejoice in His works.
(Adapted from Psalm 104)

Prayer Idea

- **Individual:** Complete the group idea below, but make a list of the places that come to mind, then pray or speak a blessing over each location personally.
- **Group:** Share with one another something of beauty from your physical locality or something that needs restoration. Keep it brief. After sharing each thing, pray as a group—thanking God for the beauty or blessing the broken situation that the beauty of God might be seen there. As we have outlined in the session, we may need to ask God to forgive that which happened there.

Use this passage as a thought starter for prayer and for blessing:

> For the creation waits in eager expectation for the children of God to be revealed. For the creation was subjected to frustration, not by its own choice, but by the will of the one who subjected it, in hope that the creation itself will be liberated from its bondage to decay and brought into the freedom and glory of the children of God. (Rom. 8:19–21)

Life Activity

When you get up from this study and before the next session, take this verse as your watchword:

> In every place where I cause my name to be remembered I will come to you and bless you. (Ex. 20:24 ESV)

Look for the life, beauty, creativity and generosity of God in all the physical landscapes that you see this week. Send up an 'arrow' prayer to God, thanking Him for all His manifest blessing.

As your group dismisses and you all go back to your lives, remember to speak blessing into those places that may need restoration or flourishing in their future.

If you have a garden, speak to the ground and bless it in Jesus' name, that fruitfulness may abound and the flowers, fruit or vegetables may display God's beauty and abundance.

Do not forget to keep speaking blessings over people and communities.

BLESSING PHYSICAL GROUND

Further Material for Personal Reading

Michael was close to panic as he looked at the cloudless sky and the barren ground at his feet. It hadn't rained for weeks. He knew that their stores of food were not going to last forever, and he had a wife and two little children to feed. His wife was already sacrificing some of her food for the sake of the little ones. The ground was literally as dry as dust. It would be futile to sow seeds for a crop. He would have to sell the family's goat. What grass there was had withered into small brown patches. No goat meant no milk. Death by starvation beckoned them, as it did with so many in his village at that time.

Michael was a nominal Christian on the edge of a poor, micro subsistence farming community in Africa. When a visiting Christian spoke to him about blessing the ground in Jesus' name, he was surprised. He and his wife had prayed and asked God for help at times, but he had never heard about blessing before.

Michael decided to try it. He walked over his dusty patch and spoke aloud to it, blessing it to be healthy and productive in the name of Jesus.

No one could have been more amazed than him when he arose the next morning and found the family goat happily feeding on a carpet of green grass in that very spot.

He sowed his seeds into the barren dust and up arose the fastest, most productive crop he had ever raised. When others asked for an explanation, he said that Jesus had literally been this family's Saviour, as he had blessed the ground in the name of Jesus.

When we long and pray for the inbreaking of God's kingdom on the part of the earth where we live, asking that His will should be done there as equally as it is done in heaven, it can also provoke a spiritual encounter with other, wicked agendas. Paul writes that God's kingdom doesn't exist in words but in power. It's not about a philosophy of life or political or socialist viewpoint.

God's kingdom is not of this world (John 18:36). The kingdom of God, His rule, breaks in with power to conquer other powers: the pretenders, the rulers of wickedness, the power of the air, and the demonised strength of the world. He overturns them with the power of the resurrection, destroying Satan's grip, breaking shackles, tearing down prison bars and liberating captives. He is the mighty Creator, Redeemer, Conqueror and Liberator. He wears the victor's crown and is worthy to do so. And He cares about the physical world, including the ground that sinful man has desecrated.

This is how the Message version masterly interprets some of Paul's writing to the Romans:

> I don't think there's any comparison between the present hard times and the coming good times. The created world itself can hardly wait for what's coming next. Everything in creation is being more or less held back. God reins it in until *both creation*

and all the creatures are ready and can be released at the same moment into the glorious times ahead. (Rom. 8:18–21 MSG)

When we pray for the blessings of God to be poured out and for salvation and healing to come upon the people, we must also include the blessing of physical ground.

But what does that mean, what is our warrant for doing so and how exactly should we do it? Let's look at some biblical foundations to ensure that we think clearly and biblically about these questions.

God's Intention for the Ground and the Whole Created Order

The earth is the Lord's. He designed it and made it well, declaring it to be very good (Gen. 1:10).

For in him all things were created: things in heaven and on earth, visible and invisible, whether thrones or powers or rulers or authorities; all things have been created through him and for him. (Col. 1:16)

In the beginning, God placed man in a garden of abundance and gave him authority to tend and steward the whole created order. God's intention was that the earth should display His character and beauty and demonstrate an expression of His loving care through the abundance of provision.

When Adam sinned, God cursed the land, sending Adam out of the garden and into a place of poverty, a place where the ground had to be worked and people earned their bread only by the sweat of their brow (Gen. 3:17–19). Mankind struggled, finding the burden too much, so they cried out for a deliverer to bring them rest.

Then Noah was raised up as a deliverer. ('Noah' comes from the Hebrew word *noach*, which means 'rest' or 'repose.'[3]) Following the flood, God lifted the curse from the ground, promising never to curse it again (Gen. 8:21). The rainbow was to be a reminder of His promise. The covenant was renewed, and the promise of blessing restored (Gen 9:1–17).

Moses spoke of the Promised Land in terms of the Father's promise, comparing it favourably against the arid desert land of Egypt. It was a land sustained by rain from heaven:

> It is a land the LORD your God cares for; the eyes of the LORD
> your God are continually on it from the beginning of the year to
> its end. (Deut. 11:12)

David, the man after God's own heart, held the earth in high regard, writing in Psalm 24:1 that 'the earth is the LORD's, and everything in it.' And let's read again one of David's most thrilling passages that speaks of God blessing the land and of the land's response:

> You visit the earth and water it;
>   you greatly enrich it;
> the river of God is full of water;
>   you provide their grain,
>   for so you have prepared it.
> You water its furrows abundantly,
>   settling its ridges,

softening it with showers,
 and blessing its growth.
You crown the year with your bounty;
 your wagon tracks overflow with abundance.
The pastures of the wilderness overflow,
 the hills gird themselves with joy,
the meadows clothe themselves with flocks,
 the valleys deck themselves with grain,
 they shout and sing together for joy. (Ps. 65:9–13 ESV)

Even the ground and its fruitfulness have a song to sing.

In January 1905, during the last national awakening in Wales, a baptism took place in a small town not far from where I write these words. By all accounts, it was a terrible winter's day, with storms and icy temperatures. Crowds lined the bridge and riverbanks while over ninety brave new believers were baptised. A reporter for a major newspaper wrote that 'even the rocks and spray seemed to join in the praise.' The psalmist would have loved that description and the insight it expressed. So would have Jesus, who spoke of the very stones crying out (Luke 19:40).

Responsibility and stewardship for the created order were delegated to mankind. Rather than obeying God, though, we have instead damaged the earth in our sinfulness by unjustly exploiting its resources, robbing the ground of its monetary and cultural value, mistreating the soil, destroying forests and habitats and brutalising various species to extinction. No wonder creation groans as it awaits the appearance of its redemption, the revelation of the sons of God and a new (renewed) heaven and new earth. Then 'the creation itself will be liberated from its bondage to decay and brought into the freedom and glory of the children of God' (Rom. 8:21).

Sick Ground

If God created and loves the earth—the land or physical ground—and cares for it, and if after the flood He lifted His curse from it, how can we speak of the earth being cursed or sick today? Does it make sense to speak of the ground as being sick?

In 2 Chronicles 7:14, we read the words of promise uttered by God Himself: 'If my people, who are called by my name, will humble themselves and pray and seek my face and turn from their wicked ways, then I will hear from heaven, and I will forgive their sin and heal their land.' Those words are utterly unambiguous, 'I will hear … and heal their land.' Isn't the statement that the land needs healing a proof that the land can be sick?

As we saw briefly in the video section for this session, there are several biblical causes for 'sick land.' We look more thoroughly at them here:

CURSES BROUGHT ABOUT BY ADULTERY

> The land is full of adulterers;
>> because of the curse the land lies parched
>> and the pastures in the wilderness are withered.
>> (Jer. 23:10)

CURSES BROUGHT ABOUT BY MANKIND'S BLOODSHED AND VIOLENCE

> Do not pollute the land where you are. Bloodshed pollutes the land, and atonement cannot be made for the land on which blood has been shed, except by the blood of the one who shed it. Do not defile the land where you live and where I dwell, for I, the LORD, dwell among the Israelites. (Num. 35:33–34)

CURSES BROUGHT ABOUT BY BROKEN COVENANTS

Because Israel's immorality mattered so little to her, she defiled the land and committed adultery with stone and wood. (Jer. 3:9)

I will repay them double for their wickedness and their sin, because they have defiled my land with the lifeless forms of their vile images and have filled my inheritance with their detestable idols. (Jer. 16:18)

CURSES BROUGHT ABOUT BY IMMORALITY

Do not defile yourselves in any of these ways, because this is how the nations that I am going to drive out before you became defiled. (Lev. 18:24)

CURSES BROUGHT ABOUT BY SIN WHICH DEFILES THE LAND AND INVITES JUDGEMENT

Even the land was defiled; so I punished it for its sin, and the land vomited out its inhabitants. (Lev. 18:25)

CURSES BROUGHT ABOUT BY UNFAITHFULNESS AND IDOLATRY

They sacrificed their sons
  and their daughters to false gods.
They shed innocent blood,
  the blood of their sons and daughters,
whom they sacrificed to the idols of Canaan,
  and the land was desecrated by their blood.
They defiled themselves by what they did;
  by their deeds they prostituted themselves. (Ps. 106:37–39)

It would be foolish to consider every piece of land to need healing or deliverance, unless we have a particular reason to think it may be so. Signs might include barrenness, failure, continuous disputes or a pattern of immorality. If we have a suspicion, we can do some simple research into the history of the area and look for clues. If the land is spiritually polluted, unclean, defiled or rendered fruitless through curses and judgement, there is a way forward, a way of redemption.

Blessing Physical Ground

Part of our ministry is to bless physical ground, the land. That is a component of our priestly mandate. The wider Church understands this. Rogation Sunday is an annual event in the wider Western church when there is a special focus on blessing the land, that it might be blessed and produce a fine harvest. Where I live, services are also held at the waterside nearby, and blessings are spoken over the fishing boats as well as over the fishermen.

Apart from church calendar events, we all have a role in walking blessings and/or speaking blessings over land. How do we do it?

The focus is on freedom and fruitfulness. Whether it's land and harvest, sea and the catching of fish or commerce and its ethical success and profitability, the steps are the same:

- We come into the presence of the Lord and listen to Him.
- We carry His presence onto the land.
- We minister to Him from the land and intercede for it.
- We speak intentional blessings over the land and sea for rich fruitfulness.

> For the creation waits in eager expectation for the children of
> God to be revealed. For the creation was subjected to frustration,
> not by its own choice, but by the will of the one who subjected it,
> in hope that the creation itself will be liberated from its bondage
> to decay and brought into the freedom and glory of the children
> of God. (Rom. 8:19–21)

The plan of God is to reconcile all things to Himself. The promise is that lions will lie with lambs, and the land will flourish. We can be part of the foretaste of that coming day as we bless the land.

Some Steps to Healing Physical Ground

Where we believe that physical ground might be sick, we might use the following framework in a blessing:

- Pray.
- Carry the presence of the Lord onto the physical ground.
- Prayerfully identify with the ground, meaning we represent it as priests of God and assume responsibility for its history—it's not *their* sin, but *our* sin.
- Acknowledge the sin and name it.
- Repent for the sin.
- Intercede for forgiveness, claiming and asserting God's promises about forgiveness.
- Give thanks for His promise: 'Then I will hear … and will heal their land.'

- Bless the physical ground; speaking blessings of deliverance, freedom, life and abundance into the land through the ministration of the blood of Jesus, which satisfies all of sin's punishment and brings glorious liberty.
- Ask whether there are wrongs that require confession and repentance towards others.

How will we know if the land has been healed or not? The simple answer is that it is healed when there is an invasion of peace, joy, harmony and great fruitfulness—of shalom.

The psalmist understood it like this:

> Then our sons in their youth
>   will be like well-nurtured plants,
> and our daughters will be like pillars
>   carved to adorn a palace.
> Our barns will be filled
>   with every kind of provision.
> Our sheep will increase by thousands,
>   by tens of thousands in our fields;
>   our oxen will draw heavy loads.
> There will be no breaching of walls,
>   no going into captivity,
>   no cry of distress in our streets.
> Blessed is the people of whom this is true;
>   blessed is the people whose God is the LORD. (Ps. 144:12–15)

Before beginning to do blessing and the releasing of sick ground, we need to be sure of our authority. Let's look at the authority of Jesus.

The Authority of Jesus

The Words of Jesus Carry Authority

Jesus is the author of life itself. He is the Father's incarnate Word who spoke creation into being (John 1:3). He speaks with his Father's authority. Even when He spoke and taught on earth, the people were aware of how full of authority He was: 'When Jesus had finished saying these things, the crowds were amazed at his teaching, because *he taught as one who had authority*, and not as their teachers of the law' (Matt. 7:28–29).

Matthew reminds his readers throughout chapters 8 and 9 that Jesus' coming was not merely for the declaration of His Father's words, but it was also for the demonstration of His Father's works and authority in creation. As we seek to understand the ministry of blessing and our role in proclaiming the life of the kingdom, we would do well to grasp hold of Matthew's litany of miracles and what it says of Jesus' authority and intent, because that is part of the backstory of blessing.

Jesus Demonstrates That He Has Authority to Heal the Sick

On what basis did the leper come to Jesus seeking healing, and from where did he get his confidence? '*If you are willing, you can* make me clean' (Mark 1:40). He recognised the authority of Jesus, whose response was immediate. 'I am willing.... Be clean'" (Mark 1:41). The healing happened.

What prompted the centurion to ask for simply a word to heal his servant? 'Jesus said to him, "Shall I come and heal him?" The centurion replied, "Lord, I do not deserve to have you come under my roof. But *just say the word*, and my servant will be healed"' (Matt. 8:7–8). As a military man, the centurion knew all about authority, and he recognised the supernatural and overwhelming authority carried by Jesus. It unleashed a response of faith.

Faith comes by hearing, grasping or being seized by the Word of God in all its different expressions. Intellectual response to Scripture is important, but not enough. We need to take hold of the message and let it renew the patterns of our thinking and temper the stormy waves of our emotions.

Jesus Has Authority to Drive Out Fevers and Demons

> When Jesus came into Peter's house, he saw Peter's mother-in-law lying in bed with a fever. He touched her hand and the fever left her, and she got up and began to wait on him.
>
> When evening came, many who were demon-possessed were brought to him, and *he drove out the spirits with a word and healed all who were ill*. (Matt. 8:14–16)

Jesus' authority is more extensive than physical healing only. As He meets the demonised, He casts the spirits out. There were many travelling Jewish exorcists at the time. They would engage the demons in conversation laced with strange liturgies and disgusting practices; some commentators speak of them using bribery, cajoling and bargaining. Jesus was different. No discussion or compromises from Him. He banished the demons with a word (Matt. 8:16), and the people marvelled, saying, 'What is this? A new teaching—and with authority! *He even gives orders to* [not negotiates with] impure spirits and *they obey him*' (Mark 1:27).

Jesus Has Authority to Forgive Sins on Earth

Jesus' authority is expressed in every sphere, and one of those spheres is forgiveness. Before healing the man let down through the roof, Jesus told him that his sins were forgiven. The man came for physical healing and received it and spiritual healing as well. When Jesus 'dared' proclaim the forgiveness of sins, something only God could do, it was a challenge to the religious leaders of the day. Jesus reminded them that His authority to exercise healing stemmed from His authority as the Son of Man, and that He could both heal illnesses and forgive sins.

> 'Which is easier: to say, "Your sins are forgiven," or to say, "Get up and walk"? But I want you to know that the Son of Man has authority on earth to forgive sins.' So he said to the paralysed man, 'Get up, take your mat and go home.' Then the man got up and went home. When the crowd saw this, they were filled with awe; and they praised God, who had given such authority to man. (Matt. 9:5–8)

Jesus Has Authority over the Forces of Nature

Though His disciples—some of them experienced sailors—were afraid, Jesus rebuked the storm and calmed the waves speaking the same word He had used to cast out demons. Colloquially, we might say He told the storm to 'Shut up!' The men questioned and marvelled: 'What kind of man is this? Even *the winds and the waves obey him!*' (Matt. 8:27).

Jesus could do only the works He saw the Father doing. Therefore, when we see the works of Jesus, we see clearly what God is doing. Jesus holds ultimate authority. His authority is overwhelming, and it is final.

The Authority Given Us

What authority has the Lord given us, and how can we take hold of it? Are these merely things that Jesus could do, or should we expect that we could see God at work through us as well? Jesus made this very clear: 'Very truly I tell you, whoever believes in me will do the works I have been doing, and they will do even greater things than these, because I am going to the Father' (John 14:12).

Jesus stated, as He healed the man let down through the roof, that a new day of the kingdom was dawning. Everyday people will soon do extraordinary miracles in ordinary places. Ordinary people will pronounce forgiveness, blessing, healing, freedom and wholeness. The glory of God is going to dwell amongst the people. God is going to 'tabernacle' in everyday people. We are the new temples: 'Do you not know that your bodies are temples of the Holy Spirit, who is in you, whom you have received from God? You are not your own' (1 Cor. 6:19).

We are learners, aware of feeling powerless and ineffective, seeking to understand how we might imitate Jesus. That's probably how the twelve and the seventy-two felt when Jesus sent them out in pairs to imitate the words and works that they had seen Him do. He was sending them out to reproduce and multiply His ministry, but they carried fear, insecurity and powerlessness compared to Him.

When Jesus commissioned the twelve, He delegated both *power* and *authority* to them over all demons and to cure diseases, sending them out to proclaim the kingdom of God and to heal (Luke 9:1–2). Jesus gave His power and His authority as the essential equipment in order that they could speak His words and do His works. Although the gospel writers did not mention such a transference to the seventy-two, it must have happened, because they returned with great excitement, saying, 'Lord, even the demons submit to us in your name' (Luke 10:17).

> Everyday people will soon do extraordinary miracles in ordinary places. Ordinary people will pronounce forgiveness, blessing, healing, freedom and wholeness.

We may feel that we are merely the audience in the theatre of God's salvation, but He wants to commission us and delegate His power and authority to us, enabling us to be actors for Him in the divine drama. God gives us the power and authority to be envoys, ambassadors and heralds of His love, peace and power. What does that mean for you and me? He will give us discernment, a commission for our locality and words to speak that reflect His heart.

> For God was pleased to have all his fullness dwell in him, and through him to reconcile to himself all things, whether things on earth or things in heaven, by making peace through his blood, shed on the cross. (Col. 1:19–20)

This is why we also bless the physical ground. God is calling every aspect of creation back towards the shalom that He desires. This is probably the least recognised part of the ministry of blessing.

Walking the Land to Declare the Intent of God for That Place

The border between Wales and its relatively huge neighbour, England, has not always been a peaceful one over the centuries. The relationship has a long history of bloodshed, and there are genuine reasons on both sides for suspicion, frustration and even anger.

Running along the border is a long-distance footpath over about 186 miles of challenging ground. Daphne has walked it twice; the first time was with friends, for fun; the second time was with a team, to bless the border.

Temporary prayer houses were set up on both sides of the border for the length of the trail. The team carried a hollowed-out oak baton during their journey. Half the wood was from Wales and the other half was from England. The baton unscrewed, and inside was a manuscript which I had been asked to prepare with a blessing on it. Daphne, who was leading the team, crisscrossed the border each day, blessing the ground and 'stitching together' the torn nations. Once they arrived at their daily venue, the baton was passed to the person in the prayer house that received them.

At the appropriate time, the blessing of the Lord was declared across the border. Cursing was replaced with blessing. Wales continually blessed England, and England continually blessed Wales. Although the idea was that the temporary prayer houses would then be dismantled, many of the participants were so impacted that they kept the houses going with blessing.

There was a great service of commissioning at the commencement of the walk, and one of thanksgiving and declaration at the end.

A few months later, a friend sent us an interesting newspaper article. It informed us that something unique had taken place as local government bodies from both sides had agreed to form a new cross-border initiative to improve the economic and social welfare of the people who lived on either side of the border.

When God established Abraham in Canaan, He told him to explore where He had sent him: 'Go, walk through the length and breadth of the land, for I am giving it to you' (Gen. 13:14–17).

God instructed him to walk the land. What was Abraham doing as he walked the land: claiming, praying, thanking, dreaming, blessing? Probably all these things and much more beside.

You and I are inheritors of the blessings of Abraham. Let's emulate him as we go and explore the land for the sake of the present-and-coming kingdom, proclaiming the year of the Lord's favour and the day of vengeance on the demonic root of sin. Then the earth will indeed display the glory of God with joy, liberty and wondrous abundance.

God's plan is that we will live new lives and discover the joys and challenges of being disciples alongside others, as we will see in the next session.

PART III

THE
WAY OF
BLESSING

A NEW LIFE AND A NEW COMMUNITY

Gather with your group. When everyone is comfortable, work through the material below. Go slowly and reflectively. Honour each other's comments. Watch the video at the recommended point, then continue working through the questions together.

Scripture

> Jesus gave them this answer: 'Very truly I tell you, the Son can do nothing by himself; he can do only what he sees his Father doing, because whatever the Father does the Son also does.' (John 5:19)

Prayer

- **Individual:** Speak out the following prayer.
- **Group:** For the following prayer, the leader will read the lines in lighter text, inviting the whole group to declare together the bold lines.

We see Jesus binding up the brokenhearted.

Give us the compassion of the Father.

We see Jesus sharing living water at the well.

Quench our thirst from the well that never runs dry.

We see Jesus eating at the wrong tables, with the wrong people.

Take us to the places where the Spirit is at work.

We see Jesus walking on the water.

Provoke within us faith for the impossible.

We see Jesus weeping over Jerusalem.

Break our hearts with the things that break Yours.

We see Jesus speaking life into a child.

Empower us to be apostles of mercy to young and old.

We see Jesus setting captives free.

Give us songs of deliverance.

We see Jesus hanging on the cross.

Forgive us our sins as we forgive others.

We see the risen Jesus on the seashore, cooking fish.

Send us Your resurrection power for our everyday encounters.

We see Jesus.

We see Jesus.

Suggested statement from the group leader: 'Today, we will reflect on the new community of blessing that God has called us to be. What might it look like and how did Jesus describe it? Roy Godwin has some teaching that will help us reflect on this.'

Play Video: SESSION SEVEN

We encourage you to take notes as you watch the video. Feel free to use the space under the Your Notes header following this paragraph. Note anything that you find especially helpful or provokes you to examine the way you view what it means to love God and follow Jesus in the world today.

Your Notes

Review

What helped or provoked you in what Roy shared in the video? Underline the key points in the notes you made. If you are part of a group, share together, if that would be helpful.

Reflect

Do you have any additional insights about living the life of blessing? What Scripture stories, verses or principles spring to your mind as you reflect on this topic? Write them in your notes. If you are part of a group, share together, if that would be helpful.

Focus

- **Individual:** The following Key Insights section provides supporting scriptures and a deeper look into the content of this session to supplement what you have already noted.
- **Group:** If you're studying as a group, your group leader will now summarise some of the things you have shared together. Be ready to note any additional points he or she may make that could be helpful to you. The following Key Insights section provides supporting scriptures and a deeper look into the content of this session. Use this material to supplement what you have already noted and to aid further discussion. You may find it useful for personal reflection at a later date as well.

Key Insights

1. Jesus is our redeemer.

God's longing, God's *dream*, is that all things might be redeemed. He longs to see the broken mended, the lost found, that which Satan has messed up healed, the hopeless given a new and living hope and the hell-bound now heaven-bound.

The way this was done was exactly like the commencement of the creation story in Genesis 1, where we have the community of the Trinity present, dreaming, planning and acting. The Holy Spirit broods over the void and the Father speaks the Word (Jesus, the living Word of God).

> That which was from the beginning, which we have heard, which we have seen with our eyes, which we have looked at and our hands have touched—this we proclaim concerning the Word of life. The life appeared; we have seen it and testify to it, and we proclaim to you the eternal life, which was with the Father and has appeared to us. We proclaim to you what we have seen and heard, so that you also may have fellowship with us. And our fellowship is with the Father and with his Son, Jesus Christ. We write this to make our joy complete. (1 John 1:1–4)

There is so much in these four verses: creation, Jesus, joy, mission!

2. The community of heaven is at work in the world.

In the Gospels, we discover Jesus-made-flesh, incarnate in the visible world, empowered by the Holy Spirit, doing the Father's bidding. The words He spoke and the things He did, He did them because He did what He saw the Father doing (John 5:19).

The community of heaven is at work in the world, opening the possibility of a new creation. This is captured in the stories of the fledgling Church told in Acts 2:42–47; 4:23–31; and 4:32–35. Of particular note is the following passage:

> Now, Lord, consider their threats and enable your servants to speak your word with great boldness. Stretch out your hand to heal and perform signs and wonders through the name of your holy servant Jesus. (Acts 4:29–30)

3. The new creation is a community.

When Jesus returned to the Father, He had already formed the new community of the new creation on earth. The apostles became the models for future generations of the growing new creation, the expression of the kingdom already here though not fully here yet.

Here were some of the marks of this newly formed community:

- It was comprised of all sorts of men and women with different gifts and roles.
- People who couldn't get on with one another in the natural order of things learned to get along and even loved one another in this community of faith.
- It was marked by prayer.
- It was pastoral and emphasized mutual concern.
- They cared for the needy.

- They didn't hang on to the action for themselves but constantly delegated ministry to others.
- They trusted the Holy Spirit from start to finish.
- They spoke words and did deeds that sounded and looked remarkably like Jesus' own.
- They walked in authority.
- They were on a divine mission to speak the words and live out the acts of God in their generation.
- They walked in purity of life, hating sin and fearing judgement.
- They boldly bore witness to the risen King and His kingdom.

This is who we are called to be too. But such a community is impossible unless the presence of Jesus is in its midst.

The New Testament does not lay down clear structures for what church organisation should look like. It is the body of Jesus Himself on earth, expressed in many and varied ways. It's not an organisation but a living organism. However, there are some tasks of the church, no matter what organisational structure is adopted.

We are to:

- Walk closely with the Lord.
- Walk in loving servant fellowship with other believers.
- Watch our own lives—not just other people's!
- Pray and stay dependent on Him.
- Connect with those around us as faithful witnesses by our way of life, manner of speech and acts of compassion.
- Name the name of the Lord, because witnesses who never speak the name of Jesus are not doing their job.

Speak Redemptive Blessing

Wherever we are, we need to act as world changers by interceding for that community, whether physical or virtual, and express blessings into it.

As royal priests of God in a holy nation, the kingdom of God, we must learn to:

- Stand in His presence.
- Carry His presence out into the world.
- Speak redemptive blessing in line with the Father's heart for people, communities, regions and nations, and physical ground, thereby binding the strongman and loosening the captives of darkness, oppression and injustice.

At the heart of all that we do is the prayer that Jesus taught us and His instruction that we bless the creation and the people in it as we pray: 'Thy kingdom come. Thy will be done in earth, as it is in heaven.'

Come on—rise up where you are and be a world changer!

Your Notes

Prayer

As we conclude our study, we turn to prayer, thinking of the new creation community that God desires us to be.

You can use the following prayer and/or the prayer idea below it. This is the prayer from earlier in this session. Say it again.

- **Individual:** Slowly speak out and reflect on the following prayer, allowing yourself time to say a short prayer of your own in between the phrases.
- **Group:** For the following prayer, the leader will pause for a few moments after each bold line this time, to allow you to say your own short prayer audibly or quietly.

We see Jesus binding up the brokenhearted.

Give us the compassion of the Father.

We see Jesus sharing living water at the well.

Quench our thirst from the well that never runs dry.

We see Jesus eating at the wrong tables, with the wrong people.

Take us to the places where the Spirit is at work.

We see Jesus walking on the water.

Provoke within us faith for the impossible.

We see Jesus weeping over Jerusalem.

Break our hearts with the things that break Yours.

We see Jesus speaking life into a child.

Empower us to be apostles of mercy to young and old.

We see Jesus setting captives free.

Give us songs of deliverance.

We see Jesus hanging on the cross.

Forgive us our sins as we forgive others.

We see the risen Jesus on the seashore, cooking fish.

**Send us Your resurrection power for our everyday
encounters.**

We see Jesus.

We see Jesus.

The prayer above is a prayer activity in its own right.

Prayer Idea

- **Individual:** Using the same method as the group (see below),
slowly and reflectively focus on Jesus and come up with your own
'I see Jesus' examples.
- **Group:** If you feel confident that your group is ready for a prayer
adventure, then you might like to explore the following idea.
Ask people to speak out a 'We see Jesus' line like the ones in the
prayer above, referencing an incident from Jesus' life. Before the
group moves on, someone or the person who said the line should
respond with a line like the ones in bold above. It should be short
and a clear request to God. The whole group should respond with
an "amen" to each response line.

Life Activity

As your group dismisses and you all go back to your lives, and during the weeks to come, remember to ask God to be present with you and to bring to mind things around your community over which you can speak blessing as you go about your everyday tasks. As you pray for familiar faces and personal acquaintances, close friends and fellow workers, seize every opportunity to pronounce blessings over them as well, whether remotely or person to person.

Session 7:
Going
Deeper

A NEW LIFE AND A NEW COMMUNITY

Further Material for Personal Reading

It was very hot. We were on the coast of southern Europe, gathered with a collection of Bible college students, the college's principal and some of its staff. I was there to teach them how to become heralds of the kingdom of God in challenging places, before sending them across the Mediterranean to a spiritually hostile nation. At night, we would go onto the roof to worship and pray, watching the flicker of light on the distant horizon—night fires on African beaches, lit by would-be illegal immigrants to Europe.

How do you bring the blessing of God to a place where you don't know anyone and don't speak the language? You function as the royal priesthood. Having been into the place of meeting with God, you intentionally carry His presence by faith wherever you walk. Then you pronounce blessings in His name.

We took a practice run. We had a time of worship and prayer, crying out to God for His kingdom to come to the community we were in, for revelation of Jesus to fall upon the people and for the Holy Spirit to clothe us. Then we all walked to the local Mediterranean marketplace, a massive area of brightly coloured stores manned by people of various nationalities, colours and ethnicities. Hundreds of people thronged the streets; the noise and the smells and the heat filled our senses. Then we did as I had taught them: walking in pairs, we slowly weaved through the market, reflecting Jesus' sending of the earliest disciples out in pairs.

Unable to communicate with people through language, we blessed the streets. 'We bless you, street, in the name of Jesus, that God may cause His glory to rest upon you.' We blessed the pedestrian ways. 'We bless you in Jesus' name, that God would touch every person who walks on you, leading them to salvation. We bless you that God might raise up some of those who walk this way as mighty apostles to their families, communities and nations.'

We blessed the stallholders, many of them working illegally and sending their earnings to support their families back in Africa. 'We bless you in Jesus' name, that God might lead you into the knowledge of the only truth that can set you free.'

We blessed each individual home that lined the streets as we sauntered by: 'We bless this home in Jesus' name, that every heart might be opened to receive visions and dreams of Jesus, and that you may turn and be saved. We bless your door, that it might be open to receive those who bring news of God's salvation in Jesus.'

The next day, we sent the students off in threes, travelling at different times on different sailings to their challenging destination. They had no spare clothes, no food, no money (although one member of each triplet was in fact secretly carrying some funds for getting them out in an emergency). Their only security was their trust in the Father whose kingdom we seek first and who knows everything we need.

They came back with exciting stories to tell. One group had found their way into a remote mountain village. Hot, tired and hungry, they sat on the ground, prayed and waited. Soon a child appeared and beckoned them to follow her. They were led into a poor home where the mother was sweeping the earth floor. She tipped the family's food into three basins and gave it to them instead, preferring to go hungry themselves. The family used hand signals to explain that they could sleep on the newly brushed floor.

Despite having no language to communicate except hand signals, the three eventually understood that they'd been invited by the village to stay for a few days. They ran a holiday club for the village children and prayed for and blessed the village in Jesus' name. Jesus was visiting that little community, incarnated through the trio.

Others went to tourist areas and had divine appointments with some who spoke English as a second language. There they found a responsiveness in people's hearts.

See how this works? There was abandonment upon God, absolute dependence on Him and His promises. There was trust between team members. They prayed fervently in private but blessed openly in public.

Notice the plurality in these experiences too. We are called to fellowship and function with others. It's part of the good news: a new, relational, God-centred kingdom community is appearing on earth. In fact, it is an underground invasion of the present reality of the power and rule of Jesus Christ, and you are called to be a unique part of it and to play a unique part in it.

Please pause here to read through the group material Key Insights section from session 7 once more. Those truths are foundational to your life.

The principles at work here are simple, and we have already been looking at many of them. Here is the framework as a reminder:

- Jesus has been made flesh and walked amongst men.
- He has launched God's invading kingdom into the world by coming Himself with power and authority.
- He ministered on earth with the words, works and wonders of God's kingdom.
- He delegated His kingdom ministry *and authority* to His disciples that they might bear witness to Him.
- Through His sacrificial death, we have life.
- Despised and rejected by men, He carried away our sins, curses, shame and pain, releasing us from Satan's grip and the world's darkness. We have been set free!
- We have been adopted as God's children and granted a new and living way into His presence by Christ's sacrifice.
- We are co-heirs with Christ of the kingdom, living in the measure of its presence today while looking forward to its fullness.
- We have the Holy Spirit to help us, fill us and equip us.
- We are called into the community of the redeemed.
- We are now called to function as members of a royal priesthood and a holy nation.

Our response to the goodness of God shapes our daily commitment:

- To *stand* in His presence
- To *carry* His presence
- To *speak* blessings in His name

As we bless people and communities, regions, nations and physical ground, we are walking in God's dream for our lives. In God's design, not only are people, nations and creation being affected by this, but we ourselves are being changed in the process, from one degree of glory to another (2 Cor. 3:18).

We are called to bless communities. To fail to bless is to withdraw blessings from the recipients. We looked at Psalm 129:8 earlier. The psalmist suggested that one of the fruits of cursing people or a community was to stop speaking blessings. 'Nor do those who pass by say, "The blessing of the LORD be upon you! We bless you in the name of the LORD!"' (ESV). *If we fail to bless, we are actively withholding God's wonderful blessing from people and places by our silence.*

Once we step into the mercy of God expressed through Jesus, receiving the blessings of heaven being poured out upon us, we are expected to give away what we are receiving. An inward flow is supposed to have a matching outward flow. A balance. If anyone *believes and drinks* from Jesus, *out of his heart will flow rivers* of living water (see John 7:37–38).

Foundation 1 for Walking in the Way of Blessing: A Thankful Heart

Christians ought to be living a life of joyful celebration. We want to be people who are shaped by thankfulness and gratitude, people who find it easy to say thank You to God and who carry an attitude of thankfulness throughout their daily lives. This is a massive thread in the tapestry of grace.

The Hebrew people knew Yahweh to be consistent, gracious and merciful. The other religions of the day featured gods who were inconsistent, immoral, vengeful and unforgiving. The followers of these pagan gods were involved in a transaction—I prayed my prayer or offered my sacrifice, so now give me what I want. The people of Israel were different. They had a relational God whose steadfast love they celebrated. They enjoyed His creation and so they gave thanks. They prayed a prayer every afternoon that had eighteen verses of thankfulness.

> If we fail to bless, we are actively withholding God's wonderful blessing from people and places by our silence.

Many of the New Testament epistles open with prayers of thanks, and Jesus thanked the Father for food, revelation for the poor and marginalised and much else. Paul stood in that tradition when he commended a rhythm of thankfulness:

> Let the peace of Christ rule in your hearts, since as members of one body you were called to peace. And be thankful. Let the message of Christ dwell among you richly as you teach and admonish one another with all wisdom through psalms, hymns, and songs from the Spirit, singing to God with gratitude in your hearts. And whatever you do, whether in word or deed, do it all in the name of the Lord Jesus, giving thanks to God the Father through him. (Col. 3:15–17)

This thankfulness then leads to a life of joyful celebration. We should be people who find it easy to celebrate, because Jesus is alive and we are chosen, adopted, loved and graced with the Holy Spirit. We have an inheritance that can't be shaken, and we're walking in a foretaste of it now. The security of knowing that we are known, loved and accepted, let alone adopted, plus the fact that He is wanting to pour out blessings upon us, causes us to celebrate. Why not celebrate over just about anything you can think of that can be celebrated: birthdays, anniversaries and much more? Celebration for us generally involves food! We might sing, we'll laugh together and we'll have lots of fun celebrating.

We should be people who are looking forward to the marriage supper of the Lamb, people who celebrate the fact that we have been made children of God. We want to reflect this attitude of celebration in all that we do, as well as deliberately celebrating when milestones are reached in our lives. There's something in this communal joy that not only makes us more whole but also testifies to what God has done within us.

Celebration echoes the promises of God. The Father and Jesus love celebrating. Isaiah 25:6 tells us that one day, 'The LORD Almighty will prepare a feast of rich food for all peoples, a banquet of aged wine—the best of meats and the finest of wines.' The Bible contains numerous stories and parables that support the revelation that there is going to be a lot of feasting in the age to come.

When we celebrate the Lord's Supper, the Eucharist, it's often hard to discern in what way it might truthfully be declared a celebration at all. We seem to interpret the instruction of Jesus to remember Him as being a heavy and oppressive thing. The tendency so easily arises to lean into the religious instead of the life of celebration.

When we consider the battlefield of Calvary, we are overawed, but we mustn't stop there. If we did, we would have plenty of reasons to mourn. Failed hope, no gospel. But we go on beyond the cross to remember His triumph: an empty cross, an empty grave and an occupied throne in heaven. We remember not only that we are saved at enormous cost but also that we are saved right now! We don't deserve it—it's pure grace. How can we fail to celebrate and be thankful for such love and mercy?

Jesus worked His first public miracle at a wedding feast, changing water into wine. He told a parable about a banquet where people were invited from amongst the most marginalised groups of the day. He fed five thousand in a foretaste of the marriage supper of the Lamb. He cooked fish for His disciples after the resurrection. And He ate with all the wrong people—especially tax collectors—all the time. To say that He shocked the religious people of the day would be an understatement. Jesus would feel totally at home at our own celebrations.

We should be people who find it easy to celebrate, because Jesus is alive and we are chosen, adopted, loved and graced with the Holy Spirit.

Foundation 2 for Walking in the Way of Blessing: Prayer

This interactive book is focussed on spoken blessing. We understand ourselves to be recipients of undeserved blessings from a Father who always longs to bless His children. You and I are then commissioned to speak blessings in Jesus' name to people, communities, regions, nations and physical ground. This is all in the magnificent design of God's big dream, His eternal purpose revealed in Jesus. It's part of the metanarrative of a kingdom created, a kingdom betrayed and a kingdom won back by love.

But we must pause and remember that undergirding our priestly function of blessing lies the foundation of our prayers. If what we do is not grounded and rooted in prayer, it might be good—it might even last for a while—but in the longer term, it will wear us out and will not stand.

As the many available books, manuals and courses about prayer would attest, the prime teacher by far is Jesus Himself. He modelled a life of prayer for us, and we need to learn how to pray from Him.

Kingdom Come: The Prayers of the Kingdom

In common with countless others, my mother patiently taught me to say the Lord's Prayer by rote, and I grew up expected to recite it each bedtime and at church services.

The key words here are *rote* and *recite*. This training taught me to meet others' expectations and enabled me to participate on a Sunday, if only for a minute. What it didn't do was teach me anything whatsoever about prayer.

When the disciples, who had been raised to be orthodox and experienced believers in God, saw the prayer life of Jesus, they realised what a sizeable gap there was between their experience and that of Jesus. No wonder they cried, 'Lord, teach us to pray' (Luke 11:1). They wanted Him to take them beyond the daily prayers at the synagogue. They wanted Him to help them understand God's heart. I imagine that Jesus had been waiting awhile for that question.

His response was not that they should recite a piece of liturgy every evening in private and then collectively on the Sabbath. Rather, He used a common rabbinic teaching method of the time of giving them a skeleton, a framework, upon which they could put flesh. He didn't say—these are the *words to say*. Instead, He said—this then is *how you should pray*. It's a series of headings upon which we hang our prayers.

I'm not suggesting for a moment that there is anything wrong in praying the Lord's Prayer straight through, in private or corporately. But if we understand and explore the depth of the framework He gave us, our prayer life should mature into what Jesus had planned for us.

At the heart of the Lord's Prayer, we intercede that God's name—that is, His character, all that He is—should be on open display for all to see. We then pray that His kingdom, His righteous and beautiful rule, should break out on earth with such overwhelming power that principalities and powers are cast down, that Satan's grip on lives and communities will be broken, and that God's loving will shall be done on earth. Which part of earth? The area that we particularly relate to would be good, for starters!

We can and should be praying for people to receive dreams and visions and a revelation of Jesus to fall upon the population. We should pray that their ears might be opened to hear the wooing voice of their heavenly Father. That the eyes of their understanding might be opened. For appointments from God to mark their ways.

Such prayers are foundational, undergirding our ministry of blessing.

Prayer—privately ...

leads to ...

blessing—openly.

When we pray for the kingdom to come, as with all praying, we remember that God is faithful to His promises and powerful to keep them.

> For the Son of God, Jesus Christ, whom we proclaimed among you ... was not Yes and No, but in him it is always Yes. For all the promises of God find their Yes in him. That is why it is through him that we utter our Amen to God for his glory. (2 Cor 1:19–20 ESV)

We worship Jesus, our wounded Saviour.

> In these last days he has spoken to us by his Son, whom he appointed heir of all things, and through whom also he made the universe. The Son is the radiance of God's glory and the exact representation of his being, sustaining all things by his powerful word. (Heb. 1:2–3)

The subversive prayer words shared with the disciples refute the claim to divinity of the caesars in Rome. They are the words of the rebel Jesus, the true King, creating a new kingdom. This kingdom creed establishes a new relationship with God, asks Him to act to cause His name to represent the holiness of God in action in the world, asks again for a foretaste of heaven on earth and hints at justice in its request for daily bread. It asks God to forgive us and cause us to forgive. It seeks assistance through the hard times and temptations, and it refuses the claims of a pagan imperial power.

Worship and prayer will gladden the heart of God—but they will also shape us into carriers of blessing, bringing more than words.

Foundation 3 for Walking in the Way of Blessing: Acts of Blessing

Loving God, serving others. Four powerful words rich in meaning. Out of our love for God, as in imitation of Him, committed to seeing our lives as acts of worship, we serve and bless our communities. Being a blessing is about our lives, rooted in God's kindness towards us, being an avenue for the Holy Spirit to work and act in the lives of those we are in contact with, bringing glory to Jesus.

This includes releasing acts that bless.

Our deeds precede our words and reveal the truth and sincerity of our hearts. James warned: 'Suppose a brother or a sister is without clothes and daily food. If one of you says to them, "Go in peace; keep warm and well fed," but does nothing about their physical needs, what good is it?' (James 2:15–16). The good news of God is not simply spiritual or abstract; it has to do with the tough realities of daily life.

We were speaking in a local church's midweek gathering, and I asked the congregation whether they knew that God loved them.

'Yes,' they replied, 'we do.'

So then I asked whether they loved each other.

Again they responded with 'Yes, we do.'

I asked whether they really meant it, and again they answered in the affirmative.

'Great,' I said. 'I have heard that when a local factory closed down and people lost their jobs, it included one of your younger members.'

'Yes,' they agreed.

'I gather that he cares for his father and at the moment cannot afford to cook or shop for food or heat their home. The electricity supply has just been cut off. He cannot afford his rent. How have you responded to that need, given that you really love one another?'

Well, of course they hadn't responded at all except for praying for him. That is exactly what James was getting at. If we are going to speak blessings, we must ensure that we are also releasing practical blessing where appropriate. In this case, the penny dropped, they stepped in and helped, and over the next few years they demonstrated their love for one another by their many instances of practical blessing.

Our deeds precede our words and reveal the truth and sincerity of our hearts.

The story of a man who wheeled the bin for his frail neighbour is a perfect picture of acts that bless. He lived on a small road and didn't know anybody. He prayed for an opportunity to bless, not knowing how to connect with his neighbours. One evening, he was taking his wheeled rubbish bin to the entrance of his drive, ready for collection the next morning. He looked across to the home diagonally opposite his and saw an elderly gentleman also slowly wheeling his bin to his gate. He decided to go across and say hello, so he went over and introduced himself.

They had both lived there for many years but had never met each other before. They chatted for a bit, and then the younger man suddenly had an idea and said, 'I'd better be going back, but let me take your wheelie bin for you.'

The elderly man was very grateful and explained why. His wife was an invalid and quite ill. He had experienced several heart attacks himself, and every time he went out to move the wheelie bin, she worried that he might overexert himself and die.

The younger friend told him that he would do the bin for him every week from now on. The old man was amazed and quite emotional that anybody should bother to help him. This simple, mundane act of kindness blessed that man and his wife.

When we act in this way, people tell others, 'You'll never guess what has happened.' Eventually they may ask us, 'Why are you acting like this?' Or they perceive something in us that provokes trust and are more comfortable to talk about their life challenges and their spiritual questions. It's sometimes called permission evangelism. People ask you to tell them about your story and your beliefs. They give you permission to witness. That's exactly what did happen in this particular case.

Walking in the Way of Blessing

You and I are living at a time when God is awakening His people to walk in the way of blessing. A royal nation, a royal priesthood, is being raised up. You have come to a decisive moment in your walk: *Will you make a deliberate choice and step into this river of God's purpose for you, and from here on begin to shape your life and walk in the way of blessing?*

- Always seeking His presence
- Living in joyful thankfulness and celebration
- Connecting with others
- Praying for the kingdom to come in your personal world
- Doing acts that bless others
- *Speaking blessings over people, communities, nations and physical ground*
- Intentionally *walking* with one other person to pray together and speak blessings over people, homes, businesses and streets

Summing up:
Be agreeable, be sympathetic, be loving,
be compassionate, be humble.
That goes for all of you, no exceptions. No
retaliation. No sharp-tongued sarcasm.
Instead, *bless—that's your job, to bless.*
1 Peter 3:8–9 MSG

CONCLUSION

Where do you go from here?

Here are some suggestions, especially if you're doing this course with a group:

- Keep praying for the participants once they have completed the Blessings Course.
- Coach them to put what they have learned and experienced into practice. Maybe holding a reunion where you bless one another again would help them.
- Encourage participants to go through this course a second time. Many will discover new insights and motivations that will draw them into closer communion with God and His purposes, including the ministry of spoken blessing.

- Sharpen and focus your personal prayers for the coming in of the kingdom, as in session 7.
- Keep speaking the blessings of God over people, communities, nations and physical ground (land).
- Commence a regular blessing walk in an area and use the Beautiful Feet outlines in session 5 to help you prepare.
- Could you run the Blessings Course with a new group of three to twelve people, including some who don't know what they believe or are nominal adherents to a different religion?
- Consider holding a free coffee morning with a free blessing on offer. You might be surprised by people's responsiveness. Talk to them, encourage them and invite them to join a group that will explore the subject of blessing.
- Do the same with a free BBQ or supper. Always stress that there will be a free blessing on offer.
- Encourage everyone who is interested to bring their partner/spouse, friends, neighbours etc.
- If you are bold enough, ask permission and then offer a free blessing in a regular coffee shop or similar.
- Don't forget: always have a follow-up strategy ready in case God opens a door for you.

Hint: When inviting uncommitted people, take them through this course but don't push them too hard to do the personal Going Deeper reading at that stage. They can do it as a follow-up if necessary. You don't want to give them indigestion. If they're willing, take them through the course a second time and ask them to invite their friends and neighbours. If they do, make the first gathering an informal meet-and-greet session. Get to know each other over coffee, then explain a little about what you are doing. Demonstrate by giving them a free blessing. Then fix a date for their first session.

The speaking of blessings is not a practice to be experimented with and then forgotten. God is renewing and restoring the ministry of blessing. If you are following Jesus, it's not optional; it's an integral part of your role as a member of the holy nation, a royal priesthood belonging to God.

Practise, practise, practise!

> **Be *doers* of the word, and not hearers**
> **only, deceiving yourselves.**
> **Be a doer who acts, and you will be blessed in your doing.**
> James 1:22, 25 ESV

NOTES

1. 'Catechism of the Catholic Church: Second Edition,' St Charles Borromeo Catholic Church, accessed February 7, 2023, www.scborromeo.org/ccc/para/1669.htm.

2. 'The Caleb Prayer for Wales,' adopted by many other nations, © Roy Godwin.

3. Simone Scully, 'Noah Name Meaning,' Verywell Family, September 26, 2021, www.verywellfamily.com/noah-name-meaning-origin-popularity-5179444.

BIBLE CREDITS

ABOUT THE AUTHOR

When the Lord called Roy and Daphne Godwin to lead a remote hillside retreat in West Wales, neither of them were impressed. However, the Lord met them there in a remarkable fashion. A deep move of God commenced which lasted for about fifteen years. Thousands were drawn to visit from around the world without social media or advertising. Many had direct encounters with Jesus that powerfully impacted or changed their lives. Hundreds were healed physically, spiritually and emotionally.

Roy and Daphne were powerfully impacted themselves during the twenty years they were there, and they can never be the same again.

Roy is the founder and leader of Roy Godwin Ministries. He speaks internationally about the good news of the kingdom of God and works to resource and equip others who are working in the harvest. As well as authoring books, such as *The Grace Outpouring*, he is the founder of the global Local Houses of Prayer movement and of *The Blessings Course*.

For more, visit roygodwin.org.

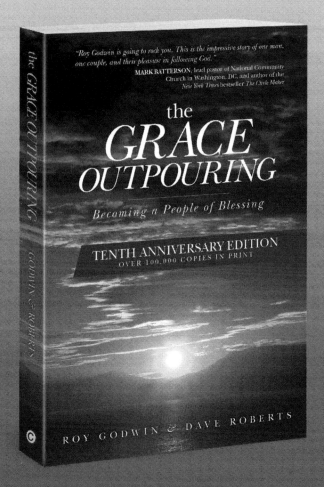

Watch God at Work

When Roy Godwin turned his back on a lucrative consulting job to lead the quiet retreat center Ffald-y-Brenin, he wasn't sure what was next. Then God showed up.

The Grace Outpouring will inspire you with true stories of God at work in an ordinary, converted hill farm in southwest Wales. It will also challenge you to welcome God's finished work into your community.